Microform, video and electronic media librarianship

S. John Teague, BSc (Econ), FLA, FRSA
Librarian Emeritus, The City University, London

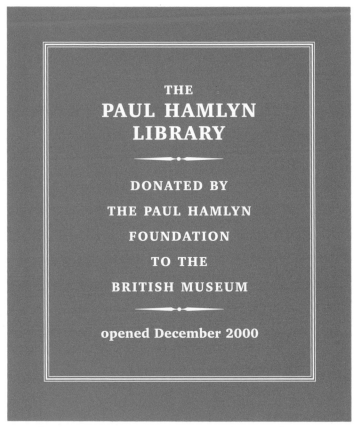

Butterworths
London Boston Durban Singapore Sydney Toronto Wellington

First published, 1985

© Butterworths & Co. (Publishers) Ltd, 1985

British Library Cataloguing in Publication Data

Teague, S. John
  Microform, video and electronic media
  librarianship.
  1. Libraries — Special collections — Microforms
  I. Title
  025.17'94   Z692.M5

  ISBN 0-408-01401-6

British Library Cataloguing in Publication Data

Library of Congress Cataloguing in Publication Data

Teague, Sydney John
  Microform, video and electronic media librarianship

  Includes bibliographies and index.
  1. Libraries—Special collections—Non-book materials.
  2. Libraries—Special collections—Microforms.
  3. Libraries—Special Collections—Video tapes.
  4. Libraries and electronic publishing. 5. Audi-visual
  library service. 6. Library science—Technological
  innovations. I. Title.
  Z688.N6T43   1985   026'.0253'494   84-18602
  ISBN 0-408-01401-6

Typeset by Illustrated Arts Limited, Sutton, Surrey
Printed and bound by The Garden City Press Ltd, Letchworth, Herts

Preface

When the first edition of my book *Microform Librarianship* appeared in 1977 two things became apparent. One was that it filled a gap in library literature, as was confirmed with the need for a second edition in 1979. Secondly, the choice of the word *microform*, when others were referring to *microfilm*, encompassed the trend away from the unpopular open-reel microfilm to microfiche.

Now, with proponents of video and electronic technologies taking over the earlier role of the wilder advocates of microfilm in forecasting the end of libraries, I offer the librarian and the library school student a new book as a guide to the librarianship of these newer media. This has, I hope, a similar practical realistic approach to that of *Microform Librarianship*, although incorporating much thoroughly revised material from the earlier book which it supersedes.

For our purposes, the term microform could be held to embrace all those media that store information of various kinds in reduced format, whether they be originated photographically, electronically, or by one of the video technologies. Common use, however, presently restricts the word microform to those media with a photographic basis and so, in the interest of clarity, I have named the other forms in the title.

S.J.T.

Contents

List of Figures

One

Introduction

Librarianship, a multi-media profession

Librarianship may be defined as that professional activity which is concerned with information — its acquisition, storage, organisation for use, and its supply to the enquirer. Although the book, the *codex* format, has been with us since its great superiority to the *volumen*, or roll, came to be obvious after centuries of use, the invention of printing from moveable type around 1454 marked the beginning of the establishment of the book as overwhelmingly *the* physical format of the contents of libraries.

There have been apologists and promoters of the *microform* who have erroneously forecast the end of libraries as we know them and there will be such advocates for each new format thrown up by developing technology. Such are the varied excellencies and shortcomings of each format, however, and such is the need for guidance in the best use of each, that libraries will certainly continue to exist and they will house an ever widening variety of information transfer devices.

In addition to books, pamphlets, manuscripts ancient and modern, maps, prints and plans, the library media include microforms, slides, films, film-loops, video discs, video tapes, audio discs, audio tapes, magnetic tapes and discs for micro-, mini- and mainframe computers, and all the electronic and optical technology based equipment with which to read the information stored on them.

The professional techniques involved in organising all these materials for use is librarianship. In so far as librarians, and, of course, schools of librarianship, are aware of this vital fact and continually update their knowledge and expertise, there is no need to fear that new computer and electronics based information professions will emerge to take over the role of the librarian. Even with home based extensions of the electronic office concept adapted to academic information, I am confident that the library as the storehouse, distribution centre and reference workshop for all information needs has a vital continuing role.

Technical exposition of any of the existing and newly burgeoning types of information technology is no part of the purpose of this book — reading periodical publications in these fields is the best method for keeping up to date. The purpose of this book is to provide a guide for the librarian in all types of library. A non-technical guide embracing the practical approach to selection, acquisition and usage of microforms and the newer media, with no particular advocacy of any medium as a panacea for all library problems. I am certain that not only will libraries remain and further develop as multi-media information suppliers, but that converging technologies will ensure mixed-media applications in growing profusion, e.g., electronic-video, electronic-photographic, print-photographic, audio-visual, etc.

Microforms and microform librarianship

Microform material in libraries is simply information — textual, illustrative, tabular — stored in reduced size on photographic film. There is nothing new about it and libraries have for many years had growing microform collections. What is new is the current growth rate in microform availability and acquisition. There is a thriving micropublishing industry; the long established major source, University Microfilms International, has been joined by an active and highly professional European and especially British micropublishing industry. Micropublishers and their output are discussed in chapter 4.

The film stock present in libraries is usually black and white. Colour film has been slow in becoming established in micro-publishing and was still, in 1983, being sent to America for processing into coloured microfiche. What differentiates library microforms from the film in one's own camera, apart from the lack of perforations for the camera sprocket, is the size of the images; the film itself might well be the same size (35 mm). The reduction of the image is normally between 1/16th and 1/24th of the original. Library microforms are commonly 35 mm or 16 mm film but can be 105 mm cut into sheets (fiches), each very approximately 4 in × 6 in (105 mm × 148 mm) containing 98 or 60 frames. There have also been some other microfiche sizes utilised in the past.

Ultrafiche is similar to microfiche, but has a very high reduction ratio of 150 to 200 times and contains up to 3000 pages on a piece of film 4 in × 6 in (105 mm × 148 mm). There is not likely to be any growth in the use of ultrafiche in libraries for reasons outlined in chapter 2. Greater condensation is, of course, readily achieved and manufacturers could well, quite wrongly, promote higher reduction ratios for greater space saving. The fact is that the reduction ratios at present in general use are those likely to give the best results and *International Standards* exist that can be specified for their production. These matters are fully discussed in chapter 9.

Aperture cards have been developed from standard punched cards $3\frac{1}{4}$ in $\times$ $7\frac{3}{10}$ in (82 mm $\times$ 186 mm) and differ from ordinary punched cards by having a frame, or frames, of film set into them in the aperture or apertures. Thus they can be mechanically or hand sorted, bear eye-legible details and have data stored at reduction on the film inserts. Film and microfiche can have optical or electronic sorting markings on them to enable mechanical or electronic retrieval and some microfiche retrieval devices involve the addition of a coded metal strip to each fiche. Film can also be in cartridges or cassettes for retrieval on dedicated reading and copying equipment.

There are two opaque microformats at present in libraries, and, for various reasons outlined in chapter 2, it is unlikely that there will be others. These are *Microprint*, 6 in $\times$ 9 in (152 mm $\times$ 229 mm) cards produced by offset lithography and *Microcards* photographically produced on 3 in $\times$ 5 in (76 mm $\times$ 127 mm) cards.

Fiche-books — bound volumes with both a printed book element and a microfiche component and synoptic journals — printed periodicals carrying summary articles with the full articles contained on microfiche within them — or full printed articles with additional data on microfiche, are other prevalent types of library microform material and are discussed in chapters 2 and 3 respectively.

Computer output microfiche library catalogues, which became the norm in Britain in the late 1970s are the subject of chapter 5.

Other non-book media in libraries

Other non-book material in libraries will increasingly be in either the tape or disc formats with which we are all becoming familiar. Whether these formats are video or audio, or both, the information will be stored in digital or analogue mode rather than as an actual direct miniaturisation as is the case with microphotography. Digital, in this context, means 'based on counting numbers' and, in the case of the binary system, using only two symbols 'one' and 'nought' or 'on' and 'off', manipulated into large numbers of combinations standing for the data one is handling. Analogue, also in this context, means that in the same way that temperature variations can be determined by their effect on the length of a column of mercury (its changes in length being analogous to the changes in temperature) so we can use variations in current, voltage, resistance, polarity, reflectance, or whatever, to represent our data in 'micro' storage, and not the data itself.

Video formats with library applications are outlined in chapter 8.

However, it is expected that full-text video disc information storage will not be general in libraries before the turn of the century.

This is not to say that there will not be some video disc usage in libraries before then, but there are sound reasons for believing that *general* adoption of *full-text* information storage and retrieval using video disc (the surrogate library on disc) will be slow in development and slower in gaining acceptance. These reasons relate to:

1. The **unit cost** both in preparation, editing and recording and in pressing master discs at in excess of £2000 each;
2. The **equipment costs**, because high density storage requires multiple access points in the library, each at a microcomputer, as well as print-out equipment and multiple copies of video discs;
3. **Technical problems** of definition, screen capacity and longevity of materials;
4. **Possible low usage** as evidenced by under-utilisation of much existing non-book material in libraries, e.g. programmed learning machines, video tapes, film-strips, and on-line services, when compared with usage of printed services, which is related to:
5. **Reader resistance** to anything more difficult to study than print on paper;
6. **Copyright problems** involved in getting agreement to publish on disc the full texts that libraries require, and,
7. The **Royalties payable** for such use.

A brief history of microforms

The science upon which photography is based was initiated by a discovery of 1556, namely, that chloride of silver darkened when exposed to sunlight. The technique of photography, that is the ability to reproduce desired images upon prepared surfaces by the influence of light, may be said to have had its origins in 1816 when Niepce, later the partner of Daguerre, successfully made the first daguerreotype prints. A daguerreotype is a direct positive photographic image and is named after L. J. M. Daguerre who published such photographs in Paris in 1839. Fox Talbot announced his calotype process in 1839 and this used paper negatives sensitised by a silver solution to make prints. In the same year Sir John Herschel is said to have made first use of the word 'photograph'.

It was in 1839 that the Manchester optician and photographer, John Benjamin Dancer produced the first microphotographs on daguerreotype plates. The best coating for photographic glass plates was then still a matter for experiment. At first albumen was used and in 1848, collodion; gelatine was not used until 1871.

Dancer was not able to find a really suitable means of production of microportraits until his successful experiments with Frederick Scott Archer's wet collodion process, details of which were published in 1852. Dancer made use of it the same year and his achievement was to produce the first successful microphotographs on relatively grainless emulsion in 1853. He produced a photograph of the text of the Ten Commandments the size of a pin-head (1243 letters). It was mounted on a slide and read with the aid of a microscope. Dancer sold sets of microphotographs on microscope slides and for him can be claimed title to be the originator of practical microphotography[1].

Following an analysis by infra-red spectroscopy of two Benjamin Dancer slides supplied by L. L. Ardern, it was possible for G. Newman and G. W. W. Stevens to assert: '. . . there is no doubt that the vehicle of both these slides is collodion'[2]. Dancer also reduced all 560 pages of Queckett's *Treatise on the Microscope* to one microform of ⅜ in × ⅜ in (10 mm × 10 mm). Dancer used the term 'microscopic photographs' — the word 'microphotograph' was probably first used by George Shadbolt in 1854[3]. It is of interest to note that, in 1963, the Library Association and the Manchester Photographic Society were jointly responsible for the erection of a commemorative plaque on the site of Dancer's Manchester premises which he occupied during the period 1841–1880. Dancer probably did not invent any new photographic process but devised new applications of known techniques; particularly those of Daguerre and Fox Talbot[3].

The *Athenaeum* of 1853 carried the first proposal known to be recorded, outlining the idea of micropublication. Sir John Herschel and John Stewart discussed microscopic editions of works of reference, maps, atlases, logarithmic tables, etc. The next notable event in the history of microphotography was the visionary statement by Sir David Brewster in the 8th edition of *Encyclopaedia Britannica* in 1857. In Volume 14 in an entry under 'The microscope' he suggested the possibility of hiding secret information in an ink blot or full stop — a *microdot*[4]. Brewster foresaw the use of microfilm in wartime for sending concealed messages.

Soon after, René Dagron took out a patent and, using Dancer's technique, developed a microphotographic method that was used in the 1871 siege of Paris during the Franco-Prussian War. Balloons released within beleaguered Paris drifted with the prevailing wind over enemy lines to French army positions. In due course they carried Paris-based racing pigeons, which, before being released to return to their base in Paris, had microfilms inserted in small tubes attached to their tails[5]. The balloons could not return against the prevailing wind.

The dispatches were photographically reduced to 2.5 in^2 (63 mm^2) from a very large original. On receipt, the films were projected and transcribed. An illustration of a surviving Dagron film sent out of Paris in 1871 may be seen in a 1936 *Manual on methods of reproducing research materials*[6]. René Dagron's application of microphotography has proved to be one of the most efficient in the history of photography, for, some sixty years later, in 1932, Dr. Bendikson of the Huntington Library found that his film was perfect in every particular.

During the Victorian and Edwardian periods, many commercial microphotographic views were sold mounted in ivory pen-holders or manicure sets and other fancy items (see Figure 1.1). The microphotographs were secured under a Stanhope lens and were viewed held up to the light. Now becoming rare, they are known to collectors as 'Stanhopes'. Many of these were of French manufacture and some were produced and sold by Dagron.

The credit for having put forward the idea of the microfiche must go to Robert Goldschmitt and Paul Otlet. In an article in the *Bulletin of the International Institute of Bibliography* in 1906 they not only discussed the possibility of reproducing the content of books on roll microfilm, but also proposed the use of small sheets of film. These sheets were to carry headings of title, author and similar descriptive material in large print that could be read without magnification, as well as the photographically reduced text.

In including a *header strip*, this early concept of microfiche proved to be remarkably close to what was implemented in due course, but the idea was not taken up in 1906, nor when Goldschmitt and Otlet's paper was republished in 1925. Finding information on a 100-foot reel of roll-film involves accessing the whole, serially, until one finds the required frame. The microfiche concept was the most simple solution to this particular problem, but many years elapsed before it was taken up and developed.

Microphotography was used in espionage activities during the first world war. The 1924 Leica camera was a development that foreshadowed the planetary camera now used in documentary microfilming. In 1926 George McCarthy showed an American bankers' convention his *Checkograph* device. This led, in 1928, to the Eastman Kodak Company's introduction of its microfilming in banking system whereby cheques were microphotographed to assist in preventing fraud. This system used a camera that was developed into the Recordak continuous camera and from this have stemmed many modern microfilm developments.

In 1927 the Library of Congress initiated project A which involved the copying of materials relating to American history in the archives and libraries of Great Britain, France, Spain and

Figure 1.1 Victorian souvenir objects housing microform pictures, with a miniature book

Germany, but hand copying and typing were the method until the adoption, in Paris, in 1928 of the Paul Lemare camera and enlarging apparatus. Yale University experimented with the use of film for the reproduction of library materials from 1931 and the New York Public Library three or four years later. Other learned libraries were making use of photography from the early 1930s.

Some early text reductions were to a size that required only a magnifying glass to read. These, indeed, were in the tradition, but not the format or appeal, of miniature books such as the *Diamond Classics* produced by William Pickering (1796–1854), set in diamond type (which is very roughly 4½ point) and is difficult to read without a magnifying glass. Miniature books are publications normally of 2 in (51 mm) or less in height. But to go back to reduced format library material as opposed to collector's items. The *New York Times* (around 1932) experimented with a rag paper photo offset quarter size edition for archival library use. Economic factors, however, dictated a larger sale than was forthcoming from libraries. Another such reduced scale text system produced by the offset method was that used in the *Fiskoscope*. This was a hand held binocular lens equipment put to the eye in the fashion of a lorgnette. The text, specially typed and reduced to ½5th of original size, was on a strip of paper 2⅝ in wide and 23½ in long.

Atherton Seidell developed his *Filmstat* device which reduced page size to ⅒th; the result was either read with a magnifying glass or projected. Bendikson's method was to lay strips of film side by side in a printing frame to produce a positive image on paper and to read with a low power binocular microscope. In Holland, Van Iterson of Delft invented a reading device for microprints. In 1934 the *Bibliofilm* service was commenced in the US Department of Agriculture Library. Based on the co-operation of its Librarian Claribel R. Barnett, Dr. R. H. Draeger and Dr. Atherton Seidell, 35 mm film cut into strips was used to meet requests for inter-library loans. This was a far sighted scheme that might have provided a cost effective prototype alternative to national and international inter-lending schemes.

In 1935 the American Works Projects Administration used Recordak cameras for the copying of catalogue cards in the libraries of the Philadelphia Metropolitan Area. The films were then projected and copied by typists to form a regional union catalogue — a labour intensive scheme designed to combat unemployment. Also in 1935, Eugene B. Power, then working for Edwards Brothers Inc, set up a Matson camera in the British Museum Library and an extensive programme commenced of photographing books and manuscripts in that library, other national libraries, university libraries in Oxford and Cambridge and elsewhere. Soon there was serious discussion on extending Eugene Power's scheme to include the microfilming of all the titles listed in Pollard & Redgrave's *Short Title Catalogue*.

The *New York Times*, 1914–18, was made available on 35 mm unperforated 'safety' film by the Recordak division of Eastman Kodak in 1935. This move into micropublishing, together with the successful Recordak micro-reading equipment, was a landmark in the history of microforms in libraries.

Edwin Patterson was the first to publish a paper on microphotography in libraries in Britain in 1936[7]. With colleagues he promoted the application of microphotography to library purposes up to 1939[8]. After World War II he was one of those principally responsible for setting up the Council for Microphotography and Document Reproduction, which was an earlier title of the Microform Association of Great Britain[9]. In 1937, H. G. Wells spoke at the World Congress on Documentation in Paris: 'he saw in microfilm the possibility of assembling in comprehensible size and at reasonable cost the great literature and factual materials of the world — a world brain'[10].

Harvard University, in 1938, set about filming non-American newspapers and, in the same year, Eugene Power founded University Microfilms Inc. Power's purpose was to photograph rare books in order to make them more widely available to scholars. Eugene B. Power, although an American citizen, received the British award of an honorary Knighthood (KBE) in 1978, for his service to scholarship in the promotion of microfilm. In a related field he saved for Britain the Caxton *Metamorphoses of Ovid,* Books 1–9, when the Phillips manuscript was in danger of being sold abroad. More recently he played a prominent role in the purchase of Battle Abbey, the site of the Battle of Hastings, for the nation.

During the 1939–45 war many British archives were filmed by photographers employed by American libraries, sometimes under air raid conditions. At the same time, microphotographed messages and plans were, in fact, concealed in apparently innocent correspondence in 'microdots' just as Brewster had proposed in 1857. More prosaically, and probably of much more importance to the war effort, the 'Airgraph' system provided a valued means by which servicemen stationed overseas had their letters photographically reduced to be sent home by air mail.

In Britain and America after the war there was much microfilming of archives captured in Europe and Asia; subsequently the originals were returned. Dr. Atherton Seidell (1878–1961), a famous chemist, who, as previously mentioned, promoted the possibilities of microfilm as a medium in information transfer, continued his advocacy. This embraced not only aperture cards and cheap handheld viewers, but also the use of microforms in lieu of inter-library loans. He designed microfilm reading equipment and freely gave it to libraries in this period. He also played an important role in the setting up of *Index Medicus.*

Microcards were promoted in Fremont Rider's *The Scholar and the Future of the Research Library*, published in 1944. Basically he envisaged opaque microcards the same size as library catalogue cards, 3 in × 5 in (76 mm × 127 mm) with the microform text on one side and the catalogue entry and an abstract fully legible to the unaided eye on the other side. Thus his concept was an entire library housed in catalogue cabinets[11].

Subsequently he toned down his claims considerably as, of course, they were received with a marked lack of interest. The Microcard Foundation was set up to produce and sell these microforms as was Albert Boni's Readex Microprint Corporation for the production of microprint at 6 in × 9 in. The reduced print Oxford

English Dictionary and the Readex issues of the British Museum Library Catalogue are much more readily saleable products of the same technology. Microfiche was adopted by American Government agencies such as NASA in the early 1960s, and standardised in 1964 at A6 size. Though developed in 1954, COM was commercially viable from 1970 and dry laser COM recording in 1979.

In the early 1960s, photochromic micro-image ultrafiche was developed and in the 1970s the great current bibliography *Books in English* began to appear on ultrafiche. Later this format gave way to microfiche for reasons discussed in chapter 3. In January 1978 Whitaker & Sons commenced the microfiche service *British Books In Print — Microfiche Edition*. Early in 1971 the University of Toronto Press began to issue its titles in conventional printed paper format and microfiche simultaneously.

Since the 1960s there has been a growing influence of soundly based advocacy of microforms by librarians such as L. L. Ardern, formerly Deputy Librarian of the University of Strathclyde, Dr. L. J. Van der Wolk, formerly Librarian of the Technische Hogeschool of Delft and Allen B. Veaner, Librarian of the University of California at Santa Barbara. Associations such as MAGB, noted above, and its American counterpart, NMA, played their part. There has also been a growing presence in libraries of newspapers and periodicals on film, collections such as British Sessional Papers in microprint, monographs, reports and periodicals on microfiche and computer output microform catalogues. All these developments have increased the awareness of microformats by library users. Outside the library world, microform systems have proliferated in offices, banks, garages, etc.

It is, however, pertinent to ask why the microform medium has been so slow in reaching its present acceptance as a necessary increasing presence as one of the major library media. Well, to begin with, it is necessary to accept that nobody loves the microform. The impersonal, unlovely microfilm, requiring effort to read on a specially manufactured piece of equipment, will never compete with the sensuous feel of a book. Nor will it ever vie with the aesthetic reward in reading fine type beautifully imprinted on well-made paper, which in itself adds to the ease in transfer of information, positive reading enjoyment.

We need, therefore, to approach the microform as a technique, as a necessary medium that we acquire and use consciously in order to benefit from its own intrinsic qualities — never as a substitute for the book. We need to exploit the many advantages of the microform. One advantage is that careful microfilming of valuable and rare books can enable the wear occasioned by normal handling to be transferred from the book, which may be in poor condition, to the

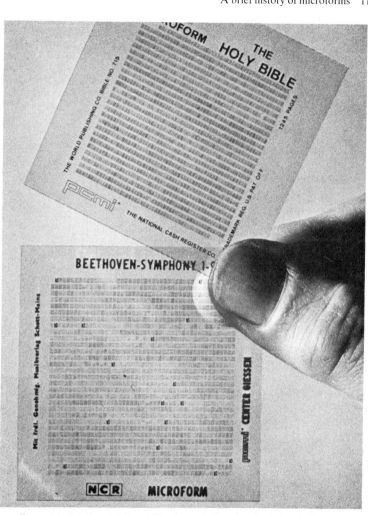

Figure 1.2 The Holy Bible and Beethoven's Symphonies 1–9 on ultrafiche

microform copy, which is expendable and replaceable. We do not need ever to regard microfilm as a replacement for the book-stock of our great libraries, but rather to see it as a vital complement offering enlargement of resource in knowledge sources, and economy in publishing, distribution and storage.

The earlier enthusiasts of the microform *per se*, in setting dates for the disappearance of libraries, of books and indeed of 'traditional' publishing, did little service to the promotion of a valuable medium; they were always so wrong. For instance, in 1963 we were told: 'the millennium has already arrived'. R. E. Stevens, writing in

Library Resources and Technical Services, went on to prophesy 'the eventual abandonment of the physical book'. These prophets were as erroneous as the more recent incautious advocates of totally computerised libraries with visual display unit output. These in turn have been followed by those who have been prematurely over-enthusiastic about the current capabilities of the video disc.

To be fair, many of the earlier over-enthusiastic promoters of the microform library concept were not experienced professional librarians. The realistic approach has been promoted and generally ignored. This has been a steady advocacy over the years of the value of microforms in libraries with a stress on (a) standardisation of film format and equipment, (b) quality control in filming, and (c) production of what the librarian requires and will buy. I believe that the current growth of micropublishing is due to its being informed and sustained by this more realistic approach.

There has been a significant number of surveys of reader reaction to microforms obviating all need for guesswork on the part of librarians, micropublishers or equipment makers on the route to developing greater acceptance of the medium. Past objections to microforms were of substance and, in so far as they are now being heeded increasingly by manufacturers and micropublishers, progress is being made.

References

1. ARDERN, L. L., *John Benjamin Dancer, the Originator of Microphotography*, 21 pp., Library Association, London (1960)
2. NEWMAN, G. and STEVENS, G. W. W., 'Analytical identification of process used for Dancer microphotographs', *Microdoc*, 17, 26–34 (1978)
3. MILLIGAN, H., 'New light on J. B. Dancer', separate reprint, 9 pp., *Mem. Proc. Manchr. Lit. Phil. Soc.*, 115 (1972–73)
4. BREWSTER, SIR D., 'The microscope', in *Encyclopaedia Britannica*, 8 ed., Vol. 14, ch. 9 (1857)
5. VERRY, H. R. and WRIGHT, G. H., *Microcopying methods*, 2 ed., 15–16, Focal Press, London (1967)
6. BINKLEY, R. C., *Manual on methods of reproducing research materials*. Edwards Bros. Inc, Ann Arbor (1936)
7. PATTERSON, E. F., 'The application of small-scale photography to library purposes', *Lib. Ass. Rec.*, 38, 347–351 (1936)
8. PATTERSON, E. F., PAGE, B. S. and SAYCE, L. A. 'Microphotography: standards in "format" storage and cataloguing', *Lib. Ass. Rec.*, 40, 212–216 (1938)
9. PLUMB, P. B., (Note in) *Microdoc*, 7, 4 (1968)
10. DAVIS, W., 'Documentation unfinished', *Microdoc*, 2, 2–5 (1963)
11. RIDER, F., *The Scholar and the future of the research library*, Hadham Press, New York (1944)

Suggestion for Further Reading

MECKLER, A. M. *Micropublishing: a history of scholarly micropublishing in America, 1938–1980.* 180 pp. Greenwood Press (1982)

Two

The place of microforms in libraries

User reaction to microforms

Surveys of user reaction to microforms in libraries reveal not just objections to the medium but rather stronger attitudes more properly regarded as resistance. Gadgetry that does not achieve its stated purpose elegantly is not acceptable; also, the book substitute concept is not tenable, for it is rather like offering a thirsty man a picture of water. In the past, there has been more than an element of both these adverse factors in microform provision for the library market.

There has also been resistance from some librarians who have ignored the availability in microform of back run serials that are consulted but rarely, buying instead bound volume sets that have taken up valuable space. They have thus damaged the library image by displaying lack of professional awareness of suitable media and fostered the impression of the dead weight of costly library provision. As these attitudes still persist in some measure, some note of the objections made in surveys of reader resistance needs to be made, before proceeding to an outline of how the situation has changed and is still changing for the better at a rapid rate.

The stated objections, in summary, relate to clarity of the original, quality of the filmed version, efficiency and standardisation of reading equipment and suitability of the reading environment. A fairly general feeling revealed in surveys of user reaction is that the user is being fobbed off with something less than he or she requested — a second-best option. The option has been exercised not by the user but by the librarian, who does not have to read the format provided. Thus the microform text is seen as a substitute book, a poor substitute at that. Indeed one librarian is on record as saying 'Personally, I must admit that I like all the advantages that microforms bring, except reading them'[1]. He saw this as the crux of the user problem, involving, at the very least, imagined inconvenience.

C. W. Christ, in a 1972 study of user attitudes and reading habits conducted at the Bell Telephone Laboratories[2], found, not surprisingly, that users required flexibility to read in the library, at home,

13

or wherever they chose. Thus his experimental group issued with microfiche reports, while showing no difference in the proportion (one quarter) of the sample who studied reports in depth whatever the format sent to them, did reveal that, of the remaining three-quarters of the sample, 43% put the microfiche aside to read later, whereas the same people had always previously at least skimmed the printed paper reports on receipt. Of the 25% who read the microfiche reports in depth, none did so at home, whereas they did read printed paper reports at home. So a change in reading behaviour was required and this built up reader resistance.

The use of portable microform readers at home, particularly microfiche readers, will be a growing habit, although they will probably not be used by travellers on public transport as some enthusiasts claim. Those of us who have had recent sustained experience of public transport will be aware that book or newspaper reading is as much as one can cope with! At the end of his survey, Mr. Christ indicated that his readers agreed to continue to receive reports on microfiche by a very narrow majority. He also found evidence that issuing the reports on microfiche did not adversely affect the reading habits of the scientists and engineers in his research establishment. Some eighty-five users participated and their demand for paper copies declined; they filed the fiche instead. The most frequent criticisms related to the poor quality of the microfiche readers and the microfiche itself, and the insufficiency of readers[2]. There has been enormous improvement in reading equipment since that survey.

Weber[1], in 1975, listed objections to microforms, ranging from varying reduction ratios through incompatible equipment and products to poor quality control during filming. Eye strain and other discomforts in viewing over long periods, poor overall screen illumination, lack of maintenance of focus in use, lack of browsing and cross-referencing facility are, in his view and mine, problems not to be ignored. He rightly saw the increasing communication between the industry and librarians as a hopeful sign for the future and the technical shortcomings of equipment should now be a problem of the past.

Stephen R. Salmon[3], writing in 1974 as Director of University of Houston Libraries, found that microforms had achieved only limited acceptance in research libraries, in the main because of user resistance. In the user surveys quoted by Mr Salmon the use of microforms was found to be inconvenient for lack of standardisation, poor filming, design faults of equipment, poor bibliographical access, etc.

Dickison[4], writing in support of microfiche, discusses possible reasons why roll film and microcards have not justified the claims of their proponents. He quotes Fremont Rider on the microcard[5]: 'the reason why the flood (of microforms into libraries) has never come is . . . that micro-reduction has never really integrated itself into library practice'. Of course microcards similarly failed to do so. Dickison goes on to state that lack of standardisation and user resistance together with difficulty in producing enlarged copies were the problems with film on open reel. It is interesting to note that the same problems, apart from lack of standardisation, beset microcard. Librarians were not only reluctant to buy all the different equipment needed to read different sizes and types of microform, as Dickison states, but also were in any case unable to afford to do so. He also reminds us that Fremont Rider, in 1944, as a basic part of his scheme, expected machines for copying from microcard easily and cheaply to become available and they did not materialise.

Lewis reported on a user study at the Boulder Laboratories Library, USA[6] and found that more than half his respondents accepted microfiche, but with reservations. Some added qualifying words or phrases such as 'reluctantly' or 'if hard copy is not available'. Very few were clearly positive in acceptance. Since the survey, the library concerned has adopted a more positive approach to microfiche provision, seeking to meet as many as possible of the objections that came up in the survey. Discomfort and inconvenience of the user of microreading apparatus were seen to be design problems capable of resolution. Many other objections could arise from limited familiarity with the medium.

Kottenstette and Dailey[7] surveyed student use of microforms and found eye strain, particularly for people wearing spectacles, a major cause of complaint, as was physical fatigue. Problems with the reading machine being unable to maintain focus were much cited, as was the difficulty of taking notes while studying a microform text.

To digress a little, some people connected with the microform industry have posited the conservatism of librarians as a *major* reason for the slow growth of adoption of microforms in libraries. It is probable that those who utter this thought are the very same who distinguish between 'active' and 'archival' microform systems, in the sense that by 'active' they mean business management systems and by 'archival' they mean library microform utilisation. The inference is that libraries are static and never develop. This unscholarly misinformed view completely misjudges the situation and, in any case, grossly underestimates the amount of activity and the continuing scope for active microform systems in archive offices. Librarians have been active in the affairs of the Microform Association of Great Britain since its inception, and the position does not differ in other countries.

The surveys of user opinion uncovered some sound reasons for the then known reluctance to use microforms in libraries. They are not all referred to above but they included the following factors:

1 **Machine design –**
   poor focus control
   poor luminance
   lack of variable luminance facility
   lack of labelled controls
   lack of accessible controls
   lack of variable screen positioning capability
2 **Photography -**
   poor photography from original
   poor copy
   imperfect text (e.g. incomplete)
3 **Bibliography –**
   poor external and internal aids to information access
4 **Format –**
   difficulty in threading film
   variety of formats
5 **Copying –**
   difficulty and/or expense in obtaining print-out
6 **Physiological –**
   eyesight and physical strain (posture) problems
7 **Environmental –**
   lack of room lighting intensity control
   lack of easy note-taking facility
   lack of microform and machine cleaning routines (dirty smeared film and lenses, screen and holding plates)

Many of these factors were always more imaginary than real: most are no longer relevant. The references at the end of this chapter relating to surveys of readers' objections date up to the mid 1970s, by which time the manufacturers were producing equipment designed to meet the earlier widespread criticism. The newer media equipment, however, often does suffer from poor design features that will gradually be rectified in a situation of keen competition. To give but one example, some visual display unit screens are too small, non adjustable for angle, and provide poor contrast. Thus the seven factors listed above can be adopted as a measure of the performance of the newer information technology media.

Whilst librarians readily accept the advice of the manufacturer that equipment for on-line information services, computerised issue systems and cataloguing microcomputers should be replaced every five years, they still retain masses of ancient microform reading equipment that should be replaced. Modern microform reading equipment is, by and large, ergonomically well conceived, designed to International Standard Specifications as to electrical, mechanical and optical characteristics. Both film manufacturers and micro-publishers comply with the appropriate International Standards. The relevant standards are given in chapter 9.

Economic advantages

What then is the place of microforms in libraries? In chapter 1 we mentioned the need to exploit the microform for its own intrinsic advantages and not to see it as a book substitute. One way of doing this is to develop the use of microforms in those areas of information provision that are hopelessly uneconomic for book production. Another area is where the information would not be generally available except for the use of the microform. A third is where time can be saved, for example, by acquiring foreign reports and theses in microfiche format that can be flown in cheaply and rapidly. A fourth is where space-saving can enable one to acquire and have readily available a complete run of a periodical publication, whereas a bound set could not be housed. Acquisition of microform copies in each of these cases can be a deliberate choice to secure advantages not available if one acquires book format only.

To use the language of economics, there is an economic advantage in microform acquisition in each of the areas enumerated above. It is in these areas that the microform medium is soundly established in libraries and not in any attempted realisation of the palpably absurd conception of the fully miniaturised library. Some people in the industry have pointed to the large and ever growing number of microform systems adopted in government, commerce and industry and have asked librarians why libraries were not being converted to one type of microfilm or other, given the obvious success of such systems in diverse organisations such as the Royal Air Force, Building Societies and British Leyland. The answer stems from the type of usage these systems have and thus the machines designed for them. They are essentially 'consultation' or 'reference' systems, where the eye is focused on the screen for relatively short periods; this does not however, mean that these systems do not have heavy usage. Library use, except for microform catalogues and data services, requires sustained reading over hours at a time.

The microformats

The range of microformats that the librarian will encounter, whilst
not very wide, comprises sufficient variants to encourage me to
draw attention to a highly significant trend toward micropublishers
supplying the particular format that the librarian prefers, in place of
the earlier attitude of 'take it or leave it, it's on 35 mm film!'. The
trend to microfiche has proved to be most strong, and, even the
oldest established micropublisher, University Microfilms International, despite its vast investment in 35 mm masters, now offers a
choice of 35 mm, 16 mm, or microfiche.

Librarians have had signal success in their demands for standardisation and a micropublisher could not now stay long in business
without being able to assert that his output conformed to named
International Standard specifications, together with giving a
replacement of faulty products guarantee. It is fairly safe to say,
however, that the whole range of sizes listed in chapter 1 is unlikely
to be met with in the majority of libraries, although the whole range
of formats will almost certainly be present. It is probably true to say
that manufacturers were originally seeking to meet the needs of
different types of user. It is obvious, for example, that drawing
office microform needs are somewhat different to those of the
library. Some variations, however, are entirely related to the
manufacturer's policy — for example, the proprietary cartridges
and cassettes of microfilm that will not fit on to a competitor
company's reading equipment. The power of the market place is
quite strong, however, and purchasing power should be effective as
a determinant of the continuance of each format.

Card, film and fiche

We must consider, then, the microformats that are likely to be
present in the stock of the typical public library system, university
library and college library. There will be microcards approximately
4 in × 6 in (105 mm × 148 mm) and some, perhaps, 3 in × 5 in (76
mm × 127 mm), and there will be microprint cards 9 in × 6 in (229
mm × 152 mm). The micro-opaques can, of course, have information stored on both sides. They have headings legible to the unaided
eye and are read in purpose-built viewers, as they rely on reflected
light, rather like the epidiascope.

Library material is still being produced on opaque microforms,
but the market as a whole now shows a preponderance of translu-
cent microforms. There are some very valuable series available in
microprint (for example, British Sessional Papers) and the Public

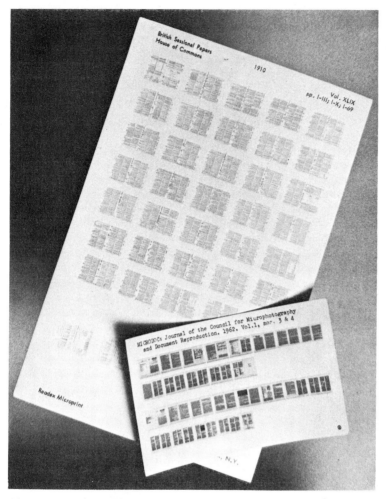

Figure 2.1 Microprint and Microcard

Record Office has available Privy Council Registers, Charles I, 1631–1637, Treasury Minute Books, 1719–1722 and 1725–1728, and one or two other items. These are still available, but as they did not sell well, the Public Record Office is not planning any further publications in micro-opaque format. The California State University and Colleges librarians have set up criteria for procurement of microforms which include: '. . the libraries will abandon the purchase of micro-opaque cards and microprint except where necessary to complete sets to support academic programs, because reliable and inexpensive printers for these materials are not available'[8].

Figure 2.2 Microfilm 16 mm and 35 mm

Just as 'card' in 'microcard' is self-explanatory, so is 'roll' or 'reel' for film. The reels will hold film usually 100 ft (30m) long and either 16 mm or 35 mm wide. These are the two sizes likely to be present in libraries. Some will be 'positive' (that is, black type and other images on a white background), while others will be 'negative' (that is, white type and other images on a black background). Roll film is unlikely to have any eye-legible titling on it and one relies on adequate labelling of storage boxes and cabinets. The film will have a 'leader', which is a blank strip of film at beginning and end to allow threading on the reel without obscuring any of the photographed images. Film is subject to scratching and can alienate the microtext user by being smeared with handling or dusty by remaining unboxed.

Microfilm is the standard format for back-runs of journals. In 35 mm size it is ideal for large originals such as newspapers and public records, e.g. census returns and parish registers in archives. 16 mm film is much used for journals and some libraries have standardised on this format. If the film stocked is negative, then the reader has the opportunity of acquiring a positive print from the film of those parts in which he is closely interested, by use of a reader-printer machine in a library. Whilst microfilm is at present the standard format for journals, microfiche is increasingly appearing in this field.

The original use of microfilm for journals probably stemmed from several sources. First, the date at which the first journals were successfully filmed; second, the convenience of the micropublishers; third, in deference to librarians who stressed the concept of maintenance of 'file-integrity', which film facilitated. Now there are considerable stores of master microfilms of periodical publications which are likely to remain in this form. In the case of journals to be filmed for the first time, microfiche format can be specified if the librarian so wishes. Also, where roll film is the format already available, the librarian can often specify microfiche, given willingness to pay the extra cost involved.

Some films in libraries will be housed in cartridges and cassettes. The purpose of both is to avoid the need for threading the film on to a spool in the reading machine. Thus there is less annoyance to the user from both the point of avoiding the task of feeding the film through and the absence of handling marks on the film and thus on the screen. The cassette type has both feed and take-up built in. Both types come in various makers' designs fitting only their own machines. Thus their purpose is narrowly commercial rather than enlightened marketing; but they can be converted.

Nowadays microfiches are certain to be encountered in libraries, because this microformat is the growth medium in micropublishing.

A microfiche is a piece of exposed film, usually 105 mm. The microfiche normally measures 105 mm by 148 mm, which is convenient in that it is not so large that film of normal thickness will curl under normal conditions. The library stock may contain some microfiches of the size 3.5 in × 4.75 in (89 mm × 120 mm), but currently they are increasingly approximately 4 in × 6 in (105 mm × 148 mm) — either positive or negative. They can be 60 or 98 frame. By 'frame' is meant one exposure of the film, that is, one page of the original book or other document or two pages if it has been filmed two pages at a time. Microfiches come in differing reduction ratios, as do other microforms.

While it is obviously possible for manufacturers to continue to produce microfiche in variant sizes, librarians can exert strong pressure towards standardisation by agreeing among themselves to purchase only standard A6 size (105 mm × 148 mm), 98 frame fiche for all newly microfilmed material from a given date reasonably advanced into the future. This relates to non-computer output microfiche. Of course there will be much 60 frame fiche in libraries, also 208 and 270 frame COM fiche, and ultrafiche with 3000 frames, discussed below.

Most microfiches are printed in horizontal mode, that is, with page following page laterally from left to right across the fiche. Thus, in a 98 frame fiche, 14 pages are displayed on the top line, then one moves it up in the reader to read the next row of pages beneath, which will be the next 14 pages of the publication in sequence, and so on for 7 rows of frames ($14 \times 7 = 98$). Although some microfiches are issued where images are in vertical format (that is, where one reads pages down the left-hand row on the fiche, then down the second row and so on), these tend to be COM fiches and are more likely to be data services or library catalogues than intensive reading material such as monographs. These two categories are discussed in later chapters.

Storage and retrieval — fiche-books

'File-integrity' of microfiche is safeguarded by the eye-legible heading that each fiche bears. An example might be JOURNAL OF PSYCHOLOGY, Vol. 9, 1940, pp. 3–85, Fiche 1 of 5. This 'title strip' or 'header' is legible against the white raised tab of its storage envelope. Now, if instead of storing loose envelopes in filing boxes, one purchases these same envelopes made up into book-bindings, a run of a particular journal can be housed in such a binding lettered on the spine with the name of the journal, plus the inclusive volume numbers contained on the fiches. The user selects the required fiche containing the volume part and pages of the original journal to which reference is to be made, merely by reading the eye-legible headings. Only one fiche can be used on the reader at a time, so the user learns to take them out one at a time, returning each to its correct place in the sequence, thus maintaining the integrity of the file.

It might be questioned why one should put fiches into envelopes bound in sets in book-bindings. It is certainly not in order to give the impression that they are books. The reason is for convenience in storing and in retrieval. Preference for the fiche over film is also a matter of convenience in retrieval of information. The problems of finding the correct place on the film, of winding back, of rethreading because one has put the film on the reading machine upside down and/or back to front are avoided.

In the case of books, reports and theses, an additional bother with film is that one needs to use only a part of a 100 ft (30 m) film for the average-length book, report or thesis. Therefore, the item required has to be searched for and retrieved from among the others. Production of such material on 98 frame fiche, however, can provide a unitary system for the whole of each average-length book, thesis or report. Where there are more than 90 or so pages, a second fiche housed in the same envelope presents no loss of ease in retrieval.

The header or title strip already referred to provides, as we have said, a statement of what is filmed thereon that is readable by the unaided eye of normal sight. The information that the librarian must have is, firstly the author's surname followed by Christian or other forenames as they appear on the printed title page of the work; secondly, the title and edition; finally the fiche number in the form 'Fiche no. 3 of 4' is essential. Indeed, all microform storage containers must be clearly labelled with similar details for ease of retrieval. Cataloguing micropublications is discussed in chapter 10.

COM, ultrafiche and aperture cards

It is probable that a library will have some COM fiches. Computer output microforms are produced directly from the computer in various ways. An obvious method is that in which the required data stored in the computer is displayed on a cathode ray tube and filmed therefrom, a page at a time. Another is where the electronic impulses in the computer store record directly on to film by an electron beam recorder. The normal reductions are 48:1 giving a 270 frame fiche and 42:1 giving a 208 frame fiche. Thus a special COM reader is required. A COM fiche reader is obviously cheaper than a motorised COM film reader and many library catalogues are now appearing in COM fiche format rather than cassetted film, particularly if the library is not over-large.

Much of the COM fiche library material will be on diazo stock. Diazo is much used in making copies in any case and is ideal in computer output microfilm, as it can be developed very rapidly and automatically by a heat process. Also, copies are in the same polarity as the original — i.e. a diazo copy of a positive will be a positive. The permanence of the image on diazo film, however, is still under research, whereas the more generally used film for library purposes, silver halide, is of proved archival quality.

Many libraries will house some ultrafiches, either early *Books in English* (discussed elsewhere) or collections of literature at high reduction, but they will be unlikely to add to them. 'Ultrafiche' means 'ultra high reduction microfiche', and in reality ultrafiches are quite simply microphotographs of microphotographs; thus 10:1 reduction reduced 20:1 will give a microphotograph 1/200 of the size of the original. The type that will be met in libraries is the NCR Ltd photochromic micro-image system.

With such high reduction ratios (of 150:1 to 200:1), it follows that a tiny scratch on an ultrafiche can obliterate a page of literature. This possible problem is satisfactorily dealt with by the manufacturers adding lamination to protect the film emulson coating. Ultrafiche has been a medium for computer-produced data services, updated regularly, with a large number of users, as, for example motor car manufacturers' parts inventories distributed world-wide to dealers and service garages. The large number of outlets made it viable but there is now considerable standardisation on to the cheaper computer output microfiche not requiring a dedicated reader.

Library stock might well include some aperture cards, although these are more commonly found in drawing offices. The standard size is 82.5 mm × 187.25 mm and by being available for punched data they are ideal for machine-sorted data systems. The aperture can house one 35 mm frame of microfilm, several 16 mm frames or a combination of each. Modern aperture card cameras such as the Imtec A 0, photograph directly on to the film — insert in a card, spray develop, spray wash and dry for immediate use.

Jacketed microfiche is a flexible device whereby a plain plastic microfiche is made up of slots or channels into which 16 mm microfilm strips or 35 mm or a combination of each, depending on the design of jacket used, can be inserted. Thus revision and updating of microfilmed information can be achieved in relatively straightforward manner.

All the fiche formats are, like film on open reels, subject to handling marks and scratches in use. Single fiches are, however, cheaper to replace than a whole reel of film.

Reduction ratios

The reduction ratio of a microform is the ratio of the linear measurement of a document to the corresponding measurement of the micro-image of that document. This is expressed as 16:1, 20:1, 24:1, etc. Thus a book page measuring 230 mm × 145 mm micro-photographed at 10:1 reduction would appear on the film as 23 mm × 14.5 mm. As a micro-image is useless unless it can be read, the microform reader has to be a device that will enlarge the micro-photograph of the document back to its full size. It is true to say that one is not absolutely hamstrung by the lack of an exact match between the reduction ratio and the magnification ratio of the reader, for an approximation will suffice.

Micropublishers should, however, avoid the mistakes of the past and aim at perfection. Standardisation of reduction ratios and reading equipment would be a very good start. If we regarded the international standard A5 sized book as the norm requiring a microform page of this to exactly fill the screen of a standard library reader, with a press button control to change lenses for reading an international standard A4 sized journal also filling the screen, the manufacturers would really be serving the library market. How far this is achieved is discussed in chapter 10.

The reduction ratio from original to microform must be stated at the beginning of each microform. The acceptable reduction ratios for ordinary library use are from 12 to 24 times. Most libraries have reading machines and reader-printers with changeable lenses in this range or fixed lenses that will enlarge one end of the range perfectly to full screen and the other end acceptably enough for use. Ideally, each reduction ratio should be catered for. The importance to the reader of a full screen, full page image cannot be over-stressed. Three-quarters of a page or two pages at once on the screen, or one not quite filling the whole screen, merely advise the reader that, in the first instance, the manufacturer of the machine and in the second two cases the micropublisher is not concerned with the readers' ease of use and acceptance of microforms, but only with his own immediate profit. Of course, if one is going to use one machine without variable lens capability, on which to read material filmed from a variety of sized originals, this same effect will result. Here the library is at fault in not providing a range of suitable reading machines.

Negative or positive

There are several factors relative to negative or positive microforms. If copies are likely to be made of any part of the microform, then a negative is desirable, as in that case a positive print will be made. However, if the likely volume of copying is negligible, a positive should be acquired. It must be borne in mind that photographs in the original publication become useless for study on negative microforms. Also, to make the reading process as comfortable and as acceptable to the library user as possible, a positive image is preferred, in that it most nearly approximates to the book. The long history of the book format makes it certain that clear black type on a white background is the most suitable reading medium for normal eyesight. There are, however, microform users who prefer negative copies, as the screen is thus mainly dark and only the text is illuminated, and this lack of glare better suits their comfort in reading.

Contrast, resolution and density

Regarding the actual text of the work, contrast, resolution and density are important factors in the quality of the microform. Good micropublishers take care of this by having quality control sections in their production lines.

Resolution, states my dictionary, is the act of rendering distinguishable, closely adjacent optic images. A resolution test chart should appear at the beginning of each microform. Readers have become familiar with resolution test charts by tuning their television sets for best resolution of the chart displayed on the screen. The standard microform resolution chart has several series of vertical and horizontal lines, evenly spaced and of even thickness in each group. What is tested is the ability of the reading machine to reproduce the original without eliding lines or blurring the edges. The smaller the series that can be clearly read, obviously the better the reproduction.

Contrast (that is, the difference between the clear and the opaque parts of the film) and density (that is, the degree of darkening approximately proportional to the mass of metallic silver or dye per unit area) together determine good resolution. The opaque parts need good density for contrast — i.e. the degree of brightness differences between adjacent parts.

Filming quality

The interests of the microform reader must be watched by the librarian. It is most irritating to find changes in orientation of individual pages in a microform of any sort. Many older viewers do not have provision for rotating the image through 90 degrees. Where some pages are photographed sideways on, the reader has either to turn the machine bodily, in the case of a portable, or to twist his head unbearably if using the heavier equipment.

Arrangement of pages must be intelligently taken care of at the time of filming. Fold-out pages must be photographed correctly to remain in the right polarity and sequence, because looking at them in sections on the screen is enough of an annoyance for the reader without additional problems arising from lack of care in micropublishing. Tabulations, graphs and charts can be repeated at each point in the text from which reference is made to them. This eases the cross-referencing-between-frames problem in microreading. References are best made in footnotes on each appropriate page, repeated as necessary. The type size of footnotes should ideally be quite near to the type size of the text. The British Standards Institution has issued *Recommendations for Preparation of Copy for Microcopying*[9], which provides guidance on this and other similar points. University and college librarians, in particular, should instruct academics in the need to produce reports and theses in such a manner that they can be microfilmed completely successfully. This BSI publication, carefully followed, will aid in this result.

It is essential that microforms of library material faithfully indicate imperfections in the original document microfilmed. The imperfections that must be noted are pages missing, wrong page numbering of the original and generally poor, faded or crumpled original text. This information must be given at the beginning of the microform, indicated at the relevant point, and it must be freely acknowledged in the promotional literature and printed indexes, etc., that go with the microform.

The features enumerated in this chapter are all matters that must be taken care of at the time of filming. They present no serious problem to the expert micropublisher who combines 'traditional' publishing expertise with good microfilming techniques. They are possible problems of which the librarian must be aware in order to achieve and maintain acceptable microreading standards.

References

1. WEBER, H. H., 'The librarian's view of microforms', *IEEE Trans. on Professional Communications*, PC–18, 168–173 (1975)
2. CHRIST, C. W., 'Microfiche: a study of user attitude, and reading habits', *J. Am. Soc. Inf. Sci.*, 23, 30–35 (1972)
3. SALMON, S. R., 'User resistance to microforms in the research library', *Microform Rev.*, 3, 194–199 (1974)
4. DICKISON, R. R., 'The scholar and the future of microfilm', *Am. Docum.*, 178–179 (1966)

5. RIDER, F., *The Scholar and the Future of the Research Library*, Hadham Press, New York (1944)
6. LEWIS, R. W., 'User's reaction to microfiche, a preliminary study', *College Res. Libr.* 31, 260–268 (1970)
7. KOTTENSTETTE, J. P. and DAILEY, K. A., *An Investigation of the Environment for Educational Microform Utilization* (ED 050–603) US Office of Education (1971)
8. California State University, Office of the Chancellor, *Criteria for the Procurement and Use of Microforms and Related Equipment by the Librarians of the California State University and Colleges*, CSU & C (1974)
9. British Standards Institution, *Recommendations for the Preparation of Copy for Microcopying*, (BS 5444:1977) 4 pp

Suggestion for Further Reading

DIAZ, A. J., *ed. Microforms in libraries: a reader.* 428 pp. Mansell Information Publishing Ltd. (1975)

Three

Micropublishing

Changes in publishing methods

Changes in publishing methods were foreshadowed by the promoters of the Project Intrex at the Massachusetts Institute of Technology in 1967. Overhage and Harman[1], in an article published in that year, predicted as follows: 'In all probability by 1975, the major publishers will be able to supply copies of most of their publications in Microform and it is highly likely that this form will replace book acquisitions, as such, to a very large measure'. They also predicted that journal publishers would publish reprints of articles using the microfiche medium. Libraries, it was thought, would buy these microform reprints only of the articles they wanted and would not continue to bind and retain complete volumes of learned journals[1].

Facsimile transmission on line, based on computer access to microform, would be the norm. Obviously we have gone only some of the way along this route. Although the scheme was realistically coupled with a proposed $15m. budget it is likely that the extra financial demands that publishers would be likely to make for use of copyright material within the system, should the scheme have any general application, was not taken into account. The final report of the Intrex Project highlighted continuing problems. Among them was the statement: 'No economical method has been found to interconnect machine-based library systems so as to provide guaranteed rapid access to the full text of documents by electronic means.'

There are elements of the predictions of Project Intrex very much in evidence in micropublishing today. Firstly, there are some monograph publications available in printed paper formats with microfiche editions as the alternative. Secondly, some new publications appear only in microform. Thirdly, some reprints appear only in microform. Fourthly, there are some periodicals available at choice in microfiche or paper. Fifthly, there are synoptic journals with the full text available only on microfiche. Finally, there are on-line services retrieving from abstracts in computer storage and some of these have source document capability retrieving from micro-

Figure 3.1 Large format microform reader (Bell & Howell)

fiche storage. Data services are dealt with in chapter 6.

If we look at each category of micropublications to be found in libraries, we can discern the merits of each for particular purposes.

Monographs

It is now generally accepted, at least by librarians of academic libraries, that many long-out-of-print books reappear in library stock in microform. Here, the microfiche is becoming the normal medium, for it is actively preferred for its simplicity in use.

Where provision in codex format is hopelessly uneconomic, we can see the real advantage in acquiring those monographs that would not be reprinted in the normal sense because of the certainty in the mind of the publisher that only a limited demand exists or is likely to exist for them. A microform reprint edition of as few as thirty copies is possible here. The publisher retains the master and a bureau or the publishing house itself makes copies for sale as required. Profit can be had from the simple enterprise in microfiche reprints of monographs. New titles for which demand will be limited can be published in microform by direct photography from good camera-ready typescripts, or from word processor or micro computer 'floppy disc' input, provided that the micropublisher is suitably equipped. Indeed modern micropublishers consider the addition to their lists of previously unpublished material to be a major part of their business.

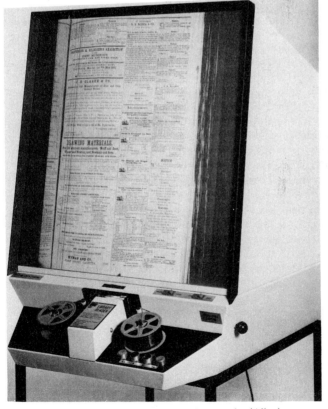

Figure 3.2 Large format microform reader (Allen)

Reference books

Sir John Herschel, in an exchange of letters with his brother-in-law, published in the *Athenaeum* in 1853, proposed that microfilm be used as a medium for the publication of major works of reference such as encyclopaedias and dictionaries.

Since it is certainly true that a reference book can be in excess of one year out of date by the time it is published, even when all due haste is made, methods that can overcome the problem of lack of currency are of great interest to publishers. The use of computer output microfilm offers a solution that should be tried in the publication of one or two major works of reference as pilot projects. If the work is programmed into the computer in the first place, however it is actually decided that it shall be printed, it can carry an updating computer output microfiche in a pocket inside the backboard of the book upon publication. Thereafter the work can be selectively and continually updated by supplying the purchaser with additional microfiches as necessary. This microform method of updating can continue until the next edition of the reference book proves necessary. Sale can be on a subscription basis and the scheme would certainly be viable for those categories of reference books where the main sales are to the library market.

It is significant that a printing industry survey of micropublishing, dated 1974, had as a main conclusion that reference books represented a likely area of microform incursion into traditional publishing preserves[2]. *The World of Learning* and *Commonwealth Universities Yearbook* are examples of the type of reference work that could well be published on microfiche and sold on a continuously updated subscription basis. Some of the larger compilations, however, are now more likely to be available in the future only online. Telephone directories are available on this basis. *Phonefiche* is the Bell & Howell continuously updated telephone directory service on microfiche. Indeed, it is difficult to see how any library can now continue to take a full national set of telephone directories in paper format when the microfiche edition is cheaper. It is an ideal microfiche application where currency is a key requirement and economy of space vital.

Reports

The publication of scientific and technical reports is very efficiently and cheaply effected on microfiche. Among the key indicators that this is the case are the nature and size of the market for reports and the ease and speed of production of microfiches.

Figure 3.3 Microfiche series and projector (Mindata)

The market for scientific and technical reports is in the main libraries and research laboratories which all possess microfiche reading equipment. There will be a relatively low number of copies of each report produced, which makes setting up in type un-economic. Electric typewriter or word processor production with formulae, tables, graphs and illustrations produced as camera-ready copy is less time-consuming than the proof-reading demanded by normal print systems other than offset photolithography from camera-ready copy. The expensive time of scientists and engineers is thus saved.

Reports of this sort depend much on their timeliness in appearing and so the greater speed in production that microfiche offers is important. A useful guide to small volume reports production is that by Williams and Broadhurst[3], and, of course, *Recommendations for the preparation of copy for microcopying*, should be consulted[4].

Government reports

The publication of the multitudinous output of governmental bodies, national and international, represents an extension into the high volume market of what has been stated above. US Federal Government agencies have led the way in microfiche publishing since 1964. The Educational Resources Information Centre (ERIC) sells microfiches of single documents or the whole output of the centre. Covering the field of education the publications of this American agency include research reports, technical papers, statistical compilations, etc.

Two similar US Government microfiche services are those of the National Technical Information Service (NTIS) and the National Space Administration (NASA). Each of these services publishes an abstracts journal as a guide to what is available. In fact these three Federal Government agencies gave great impetus to the practice of issuing reports on standard sized microfiches by their decision to issue their own publications in this way. They provided 'supply push' to a market where there was very little 'demand pull'.

Periodicals

The issue of *New Scientist* of 20 April, 1972 contained an article by G. Seeber, entitled 'Big future for the wordshrinkers?' This article was to draw attention to the fact that it was the first issue of *New Scientist* to be published simultaneously in both printed paper and microfiche editions.

The significance of this event was that it was the first large circulation weekly paper to adopt this technique. This event was rapidly followed by *New Society*, a paper from the same publisher, adopting the same publication pattern. The microfiches used are silver halide, 98 frame, 24:1 reduction. Certain learned journals were already available on microfiche as well as printed paper format, and one such was *The Philosophical Magazine*, which Kodak Ltd. were then advertising.

Since 1978, microfiche and printed paper editions of *Institute of Physics* periodicals have been published simultaneously, their last three titles being added to the list in 1983. Microfiche editions, which are priced at only 60% of the paper edition, are silver 98 frame positives. Microfiche back issues are available from 1982, but earlier years are on microfilm.

The *American Institute of Physics* makes all its own journals and those of its member societies such as the Optical Society of America, available, positive or negative, on 16 mm or 35 mm film on reel or cartridge, but not microfiche. The microform editions are mailed to subscribers shortly after publication of the printed paper editions. Complete back-runs are available and no library need have any unwanted gaps in its back-runs of physics journals.

The *Institute of Electrical and Electronics Engineers* has microfiche editions available for most of its periodicals at the same price as its printed paper issues. 50% discount can be had when microfiche copies are ordered at the same time as the standard edition. Back issues, 35 mm or 16 mm, positive or negative, on reels or cartridges, as required, are available.

The *American Mathematical Society* has its journals available in microform, 16 mm film and microfiche positives. *Mathematics of Computation* has a microfiche supplement in a pocket at the end of its printed issues. Those journals, such as *Bulletin of the American Mathematical Society*, that are published with simultaneous microfiche availability, explicitly offer the overseas subscriber microfiche by air mail to arrive much before the printed paper issues.

The activities of these major learned societies in the field of the micropublication of periodicals can be taken as typical of many others.

New Scientist on microfiche, however, has an additional attraction for librarians. Being a popular weekly printed on newsprint rather than the heavier papers used in learned journals, *New Scientist* is the sort of publication for which it is difficult to satisfactorily store and use back-runs in libraries. This sort of paper stock gets tattered in use and is not suitable for binding. Thus if the librarian can subscribe additionally to a silver halide microfiche edition for his files of this title and regard the paper issue as consumable, an advantage is gained. Foreign libraries benefit, in addition, by rapid receipt of *New Scientist* microfiche by air mail.

Generally speaking, periodical publications are ideal candidates for micropublication. Learned journals, in these days, commonly have relatively low circulation and tend to grow bulky with concomitant high paper, printing and postage costs. In some cases libraries in time become, almost exclusively, the subscribers. Journal back-runs, out of copyright, have been the staple microform input into academic libraries and the majority have been and still are on 35 mm microform. Librarians, I believe, should now abandon the fears about 'file-integrity' that led to their preference for film and adopt positive policies in acquisition of periodicals on microfiche.

The convenience of use is so much greater with fiche as compared with roll film, and file-integrity is taken care of by provision of suitable binders made up of fiche housing envelopes, or plastic holders in loose-leaf books. Users normally take out only one fiche at a time. At the point of selecting one particular fiche the user has narrowed his or her retrieval problem to the appropriate volume and is within a manageable number of pages from the item required. Fischer[5] summarised librarians' preference for microfiche over other microforms, as follows:

1. Microfiche is cheaper than cartridge-contained roll film.
2. It requires two-tenths of the space taken up by roll film.
3. Access is faster when data are stored on fiche.
4. Production of microfiche requires less time than production of roll film, a significant factor in a time-conscious system.

A leading micropublisher's case for 16 mm cartridge format for journals appeared in the *International Journal of Micrographics and Video Technology*[6]. Briefly, it relates to the convenience in use of cartridges as compared with open reel film. Whereas 35 mm film is not successfully adaptable to use in cartridges, 16 mm film is. Thus, when, in the 1970s, special libraries began to turn to microform copies of journals in order to save space, they tended to ignore the availability of 35 mm film editions. They selected 16 mm in cartridge for use on motorised reading equipment. Their needs were different from those of other libraries and for a few years they had money available to buy relatively expensive motorised readers and to pay for conversion of 35 mm film to their chosen format.

Where a periodical publisher elects to publish 'simultaneously' in microfiche and printed paper editions, as in the case of *New Scientist*, the two editions are not quite simultaneous. The reason is that the microfiche edition is filmed from the printed version. In some cases one is required to subscribe to the paper version in order to be able to acquire the microform. Where this is the case the microfiche will normally be cheaper, perhaps half the price of the printed paper periodical. The economy will come from savings in binding and storage costs.

Some periodicals in microform are available at the same price as the paper version thus giving just a choice, not an economy, at the outset. These have great value at least to overseas library subscribers who receive the microfiche very rapidly and comparatively cheaply by airmail.

Dr. Edward Gray of Microforms International Marketing Corporation and a director of Pergamon Press, in 1975 described the Pergamon Press/MIMC experiment[7]. Having tried in 1972 a simultaneous microfiche edition of more than one hundred journals sold for a subscription additional to that for the 'normal' edition, without success, in 1975 a new experiment was carried out. This involved sending a weekly microfiche of *Tetrahedron Letters* gratis to five hundred libraries which subscribed to the printed paper edition. A negative microfiche was sent to Canadian and US libraries and a positive elsewhere. This was based on the belief that machines for copying from microfiche were more prevalent in Canada and America than elsewhere in the world.

Certain libraries suggested giving up the printed issues and this had implications for the size of the print run. Thus it was decided to discontinue the experiment but to base the 1976 publishing programme on its findings. Thus from January 1976, Pergamon Press journals have been available on microfiche simultaneously with the printed paper edition. This means that all 346 journals are now available on fiche at 80% of the normal price. If the printed paper edition is subscribed to the microfiche edition is charged at 50% of the paper edition price. Whilst the microfiche is a simultaneous edition, if microfilm is chosen it comes at the end of the year. The film can be had on 16 or 35 mm open reels or Kodak or Ektamate magazines, Kodak or 3M cartridge, negative or positive. Microfiche and microfilm are sent by air.

The marketing strategy of Pergamon Press is to provide journals in the format the individual library prefers. Where the microfiche edition is sold it is assumed that libraries will make copies for internal use and the pricing structure takes this into account. It also allows that libraries expect and have the right to expect archival silver halide film and that faulty microfilm discovered even years later will be replaced without charge to the library.

Certain micropublishers have a trade-in programme whereby they encourage libraries to go over to microform provision of periodicals by offering a trade-in value for the printed paper copies to be set against the cost of microform copies.

The Journal of Wildlife Disease is published only on microfiche. Other publishers should consider the economics of publishing a periodical on microfiche alone — that is to say, without recourse to a printed paper issue at all. What are the advantages? First, one is not constrained by the need to edit the material at page proof stage into a multiple of eight pages in order to keep costs down, avoid expensive blank pages or contract the text to fit. A few blank frames on a 98 frame fiche are neither here nor there, for there is no financial loss involved and each issue of the majority of monthly journals will certainly fit on to one fiche. The preparation of copy using justified-line electric typewriters in order that the result is ready for the microfilm camera is essential for full economy here.

Bovee[8] has estimated that the economic advantage is on the side of microfiche publication, even in runs of up to 50 000 copies.

The second advantage to be noted is that if one publishes with half-tones, the economic advantage of microfiche is greater still, for its costs remain the same while those for print rise by the amount of the plate-making costs. Thirdly, the same source also points out that there are possible savings for both publisher and librarian where a print-run can be reduced, paper and printing costs saved and microfiche supplied to libraries in place of paper copies, at a lower price. This is attractive to them and the saving is added to that on binding and storage costs. This is so in the case of the Pergamon Press periodicals discussed above.

The increasing availability of periodicals in microform is assisting libraries in two ways. One is by economy in expensive space and the other is by enabling the systematic completion of back-runs of previously incompletely held titles. Thus provision is made on the spot of a much fuller service at a lower cost than would otherwise be the case. There is, too, some saving on inter-library loan costs. Current subscription to a periodical publication meets current needs; it means that a printed paper copy is available for the period of the greatest demand for its contents. If, then, instead of binding the paper copies one purchases the microform edition, the library has the best of both worlds, economising on space as well as binding costs. Keeping up to date with current literature requires browsing and scanning, for which microform does not provide the best possible facility. However, after the immediate currency of a journal the subsequent reduced volume of use involving particular articles and access via abstracts and indexes make microform a suitable medium.

Synoptic journals

What is known as the synoptic journal is no longer a publishing experiment but rather an established category of periodical publication. It cannot be said to have achieved any degree of popularity. The norm in this genre is for synopses, only, of new articles to be published in printed paper format, with the subscription charged entitling the subscriber to receive microfiche copies of the full text of any articles as required.

The paramount aim of synoptic journal publishing should always be currency of the information offered. Success in meeting this aim removes the learned society's backlog of refereed papers awaiting publication. Secondary aims include: (a) the maintenance of learned journal publishing programmes in the face of declining sales due to increased prices and library budgets that contract in real terms under inflationary conditions, and (b) profitability stemming from reduced production costs. It should be borne in mind that while microform publication represents a reduction in the browsing facility available to the library user, synoptic publication represents a gain in browsing facility. This is due to the reader's ability to skim the *whole* synoptic journal issue, thus keeping up to date in the wider, less specialist range of his or her discipline.

It is usual for the author to produce camera ready copy both of the full text and of the synopsis. Since 1977 The Royal Society of Chemistry has published the *Journal of Chemical Research*, jointly with the French and German Chemical Societies. This was a pioneer synoptic journal not a replacement for an existing publication. 'It represents a new concept in scientific publishing and is intended as the first step towards the development of a more logical system of chemical primary publications in Europe'. The journal covers all areas of chemistry and English synopses of research papers are author-produced and include key bibliographical references. The full articles are available on 98 frame silver negative fiche, or, at choice, in miniprint at 3 to 1 reduction which means nine typescript pages to each journal page.

The Institution of Mechanical Engineers produced a synoptic journal, *Engineering Synopses*, 1977–1979. This was a joint British Library experimental project with the full articles available either on microfiche or by Xerox copy. There are now synoptic journals in management, education and other fields of study.

Abstracting and indexing services

Abstracting and indexing services are a category of library material where, because of the great and ever growing volume of data each service has to carry, computer and microform techniques clearly have a role to play. Apart from economies in binding costs and space, no other financial benefit accrues to a library as a result of a decision to acquire abstracts in microform.

As computerisation is introduced specifically in order to produce the paper edition and the computer output microform edition is in some sense a competing by-product of this process, together with the fact that libraries constitute the only market, a purchase in microform means one less sale in paper format and there can be no price advantage.

Abstracting and indexing services are the subject of chapter 6.

Other data services

An example of a data service where use of microform publication techniques enables dissemination of the data in full that would otherwise have to be abstracted and indexed is the Middle East Data file (University Microfilms). Based on the input to the Durham University centre for Middle Eastern and Islamic studies, the material included is the type of useful contemporary government, commercial, political and statistical documentation that is difficult to acquire and laborious to organise for use because of varied language, format, frequency, etc. In other words, microform is the only method of publication that can keep the price within reasonable bounds. In addition, parts of such a service can be subscribed to (for example, by area or topic) to suit particular library needs.

Inter Documentation Company, of Zug, Switzerland, also have a Middle East Microfiche Project. It differs from the service described above in that not only up-to-date materials are included, but also rich historical sources which are not available otherwise except to those who have access to the libraries of the World Bank, International Labour Office, United Nations and the School of Oriental and African Studies. The microfiches are black and white positive prints, silver halide, between 14 and 20 reduction, depending on the size of the original. The whole set can be purchased, or parts by country or single titles.

Publications such as *Beilsteins Handbuch der Organischen Chemie* and *Landolt-Bornstein: Numerical Data and Functional Relationships in Science and Technology*, where scientific data are expensively compiled and sold in bound volume format over an extended or even an indefinite period, are ideal candidates for microform publication. There are readily apparent reasons for this. First, the main sale is to libraries. Secondly, the sale price per volume rapidly becomes so high as to be a positive deterrent to purchase. Now that Beilstein volumes cost some hundreds of pounds each, one can readily appreciate that in a situation where library budgets have decreased in real terms, cancellation of standing orders for this title have become commonplace. Thirdly, this situation leads to further increased charges per volume to the remaining library subscribers.

Having reached this point, the viability of publications of this type must be in question and microfiche publication should be seriously considered. It is true that the major publication costs lie in the area of the compilation and editing of such works, but nevertheless production of microfiche from camera ready copy offers substantial economies. A lower selling price and an extended library market could then re-establish viability.

Theses

The acquisition by libraries of overseas university theses is facilitated and speeded up by their ever-widening availability in microform and their listing in *Dissertation Abstracts International*. If microfiche is the chosen option airmail becomes a reasonably cheap method of rapid despatch. University Microfilms International began microfilming theses in 1938, originally those of American Universities only. Later the coverage was extended to include those foreign universities willing to co-operate.

Universities should now progress to requiring postgraduate students to deposit just one copy of their dissertations and theses for the award of higher degrees. The submitted copy should be required to be camera-ready-copy in unbound sheets to be microfilmed by the university library. It is probable that 16 mm microfilm made up into jacketed microfiche would be used. Thus the purchase of relatively expensive apparatus to produce microfiche directly could be avoided. Alternatively, a bureau could be employed to film all but those theses restricted because they contain patented or other safeguarded information.

Microform would provide a suitable method of publication in place of the expensive production of five or so bound copies of typed and xeroxed pages — an expense that falls entirely on the candidate. National libraries, of course, microfilm theses, but the real problem is the avoidance of production in book format in the first place. A university must retain a copy of each of the theses accepted for the award of its own higher degrees and is both the heaviest user of them and the place of first resort for enquiries to borrow or buy. Microform best meets these requirements.

Dissertation Abstracts On-line has now been announced as an alternative to the printed paper and microform editions of *Dissertations Abstracts International*. *Index To Theses* is a more complete listing in the case of UK Universities.

Archives

Archives now available on microfilm provide a multiplication of research material. Its geographical spread in libraries is most important in these days of increased transport costs. There is much to be done here in the expert refilming of some archives badly photographed during the 1939–45 war years. Interest in researching central and local archives is developing rapidly and microfilm is a vital aid.

School libraries might well have quite limited resources in microform; however, archival material is one area where the young can be introduced to historical disciplines in an exciting way by the use of facsimile local records, as the successful Leicestershire experiment has shown[9]. In this experiment Edwards had sections of local directories, maps and registers microfilmed, and issued microfiches and readers to schools.

Archival material is one area where librarians in all types of library are unlikely to object to micropublishers assembling collections and offering for sale the 'whole package' or individual parts of it. In general, the professional librarian does know better than the publisher what should be acquired for any given library and will resist, by expression of marked indifference, all sales promotion of a microform library of the world's classics or whatever ill-conceived encyclopaedic collection a publisher may have been moved to issue. This should not surprise publishers, because the market for such material in printed paper format has never been the libraries, but rather individuals with magpie instincts.

The collections of micropublications that are well conceived and will sell to libraries are those that are under the editorship of an expert and are based on the known needs of scholars. Harvester Press Ltd is an example of a publisher issuing such wholly acceptable series. The *Unpublished Papers of the English Civil War and Interregnum* might be cited as an example. This microfilm set includes many previously unpublished and uncalendared State Papers of the period and in reality is what the publishers claim — a major new research source. It has a booklet with introductory material and an index and is on silver halide positive microfilm. The use of microforms for archives is discussed more fully in chapter 9.

Bibliographical services

The standard general current bibliographies of publications in English early adopted microform publication. The first of these was *Books in English*, at first published on ultrafiche at 150 times reduction, but later the format was sensibly changed to microfiche.

Every bookseller worth his salt now has a microfiche viewer and subscribes to *British Books in Print* (Whitaker), 1978 to date. *British Books Out of Print* has now commenced publication. As the basis of these services is computer-held constantly amended data, they are able to provide subscribers with regularly up-dated sets of microfiche. *Books in Print* (Bowker) is another service that has become available on microfiche. Another great bibliography, The British Library *General Catalogue of Printed Books 1976–1982* on microfiche, offers, not only space economy but financial economy as well, for it is one fifth of the price of the printed and bound edition.

Catalogues

Library catalogues on computer output microfilm (COM) are the obvious solution to the growing problem of cataloguing backlogs in academic and public libraries. In place of each library cataloguing the same books, national services using machine readable records can produce a COM fiche catalogue for each library.

COM catalogues are discussed fully in chapter 5.

Ephemera

Collections of ephemera are a 'natural' field of microform library development. The difficulty of acquiring complete sets of the ephemeral publications required in social science studies and research indicates that many libraries will have incomplete sets of publications of this sort that they need on a continuing basis.

Micropublication of such packages as *Britain and Europe since 1945*, which is composed of the publications of sixty-seven political movements, groups and other publishers concerned with getting Britain into or keeping Britain out of the European Common Market, meets this need.

Complete microform libraries of 'seminal' writers

A new dimension has undoubtedly been added to publishing by a concept that is possibly only capable of achievement at the present time by micropublication. The concept is the publication of the actual library of a great thinker and writer (in so far as that library still exists as a discrete collection), as well as the various editions of the author's works, together with an introduction by a leading academic in that field of study. Thus the sources used together with annotations can be read in the context of the evolution of a theory.

Even apparently unrelated items such as the belles lettres the writer was reading at the time and ephemera from his or her library can be included. Microforms International Marketing Corporation has performed this service for students of Adam Smith, David Ricardo, John Maynard Keynes and Robert Malthus. Clearly, the sources used by these seminal writers in economics are of immense importance in gaining a better understanding of their works.

In some cases, where the libraries are dispersed, they are nevertheless well documented. Thus it is feasible to assemble the titles known to have been in a writer's library and to photograph them for inclusion in the micropublished series.

Other library materials

Many other materials that in the past might have been acquired by a given library and long remained uncatalogued and used only by those scholars fortunate enough to know of their location are now microfilmed and made available to researchers in their own libraries. These are usually microfilmed and sold by established micropublishers with royalties on sales accruing to the library.

Reputable micropublishers will always ask permission to photograph out of print, out of copyright material in the stock of a library. Librarians should always provide ground rules under which the operation may be carried out and these rules should include mention of care of the binding and, specifically, no disbinding. Rare and valuable works should be filmed only on library premises under responsible supervision.

Quite apart from the specific economic advantages accruing from the adoption of each of these types of microform material in libraries, already noted, there is the major factor that, of its nature, the microform is a cheaper medium than the printed book. It is up to librarians to see that such prices are charged that benefit libraries, allow the adequate development of the medium and provide micropublishers with a reasonable return on their investment. It is up to micropublishers to select material carefully, to employ scholarly editors and always to be willing to sell parts of sets. They can only gain by greater sales if they do sell parts of sets and thus enable the microform industry to supply markets not served in other ways.

In the next chapter the work of the leading micropublishers is surveyed. The quality of micropublications and the professional approach of micropublishers generally has been greatly enhanced as a result of the publication, in 1979, of *Microform Publishing* by Peter Ashby and Robert Campbell. To state that this work has become the established handbook is not to undervalue the activity of other leading micropublishers over the years in promoting sound practice and new ideas in publishing. Edward Gray of Microforms International Marketing Corporation to name but one, has certainly cherished similar aims.

References

1. OVERHAGE, C. F. J. and HARMAN, R. J., 'The on-line intellectual community and the information transfer system at M.I.T. in 1975', in *The Growth of Knowledge: Readings on Organization and Retrieval of Information*, ed. M. Kochen, pp. 77–95, Wiley, New York (1967)
2. MASLIN, J. M., *Micropublishing: The Present Situation*, 46 pp., PIRA, Leatherhead, (1974)

3. WILLIAMS, B. J. S. and BROADHURST, R. H. 'The use of microfiches for scientific and technical reports — considerations for the small user', Agardograph No. 198, AGARD (1974)
4. British Standards Institution. *Recommendations for the Preparation of Copy for Microcopying* (BS 5444:1977) 4 pp.
5. FISCHER, M. L., 'The use of COM at Los Angeles Public Library', *J. Micrographics*, 6, 205–210 (1973)
6. GRAY, E., The 35 mm film 'addiction', *Int. J. Micrographics and Video Technology*, 2, 4, (1983) 291–292.
7. GRAY, E., 'Subscriptions on microfiche: an irreversible trend', *J. Micrographics*, 8, 241–244 (1975)
8. BOVEE, W. G., 'Scientific and technical journals on microfiche', *IEEE Trans. on Professional Communication*, PC–16, 113–116, 178 (1973)
9. EDWARDS, R. A. P. 'Microforms in Schools', *Microdoc*, 14, 37–42 (1975)

Suggestions for Further Reading

ASHBY, P. and CAMPBELL, R. *Microform Publishing*. 189 pp. Butterworths (1979)
VEANER, A. B., *ed, Studies in Micropublishing: 1853–1976: Documentary Sources*. Microform Review/Mansell Information Publishing Ltd. (1977)

Four

Micropublishers surveyed

This survey of micropublishers makes no attempt or claim to be comprehensive, rather it seeks to be a pointer to the vast amount of material on the market with some indication of where requirements might be met.

Learned societies are not listed although they are prolific publishers of periodicals in microform, neither are periodical publishers *per se*. Some are cited in chapter 3 in relation to types of micropublication. It can be taken for granted that *any* periodical can be purchased in microform, but not always from the publisher of the original.

The current surge forward in micropublishing is, for the reasons already outlined, based on the international standard size A6 microfiche, i.e. 105 mm × 148 mm. This is usually 98 frame and the text reduction not more than 24:1. That there should be growth in micropublishing at the present time is due to a combination of circumstances. These are, among others, the development of expertise, materials and equipment in the photographic industry to date, the degree of acceptance already achieved and the very high cost of paper, printing, postage and storage for printed paper editions.

Monographs of limited marketing possibilities, that is to say worthwhile works of under one hundred pages, where a necessarily low selling price will so depress the publisher's possible return that he will not publish on paper, can be published in an economically viable way on microfiche. Monographs of likely limited circulation, whatever their length, are obviously suitably produced on microfiche.

One would not suggest publishing popular works in this way at the present time thus arbitrarily limiting their sale to libraries. Indeed it cannot be asserted that microforms are, in every case, cheaper to produce than are printed books. It should be remembered that printing involving long runs can achieve a progressively cheaper cost per copy within limits, for the comparatively high setting-up costs are spread over more copies. Microform publications are subject to the same sort of costs in promoting sales as are books, but each additional microform produced adds the same additional production costs to the total, and there are diminishing returns. Thus the economic advantage in microform publishing lies in the area of low production runs.

Undoubtedly it makes sense for booksellers to stock and sell microform-reading apparatus once they start selling the microforms. There has been a certain lack of enterprise here. However, the 1978 adoption of the microfiche format by J. Whitaker & Sons Ltd for *British Books in Print* has been readily supported by booksellers and thus computer output microfiche readers are now commonplace in bookshops.

The annual exhibition of Specialist Publishers in London (SPEX) has a small but growing representation of micropublishers, and, since 1976, has offered them special facilities. This does something to foster the view that publishing is publishing regardless of the fact that some of it takes place in microform.

All publications should be listed in the general current bibliographies regardless of their format. The entry in the bibliography must indicate which are microforms and state whether they are microfiche, microprint, microcard or microfilm, and if film, the size and number of reels or cassettes. Fiche books have the advantage that they can more readily be listed and sold with other books. If they carry a microfiche in colour, then the colour is, at the very least, as faithful a record as colour printing, but is likely to be better. Low run editions of fiche books is the norm. Sheets of the printed text can be stored and 'on-demand' copies of the colour microfiche can be made up and copies bound up in small batches.

Bell & Howell Ltd., Micromedia Division, Telford Road, Bicester, Oxford OX6 0UP

The trend to microfiche is followed by Bell & Howell with the issue of a catalogue of over 700 periodicals and newspapers available on microfiche. For those librarians who remain committed to 35 mm open reel microfilm, there is a separate catalogue. The microfilm catalogue is much larger, including in its listing the original products of the American parent company. Bell & Howell claim to have more than 7000 titles listed and the catalogue gives full availability details of 150 American newspapers. Both catalogues are available on microfiche. Whereas the Index to the *Times* may well be adequate as a guide to the historical content of British newspapers in general, as well as the *Times* in particular, to study the USA with its vast area and regional life style, one needs indexes to many important newspapers. Bell & Howell are meeting this need, independently preparing and publishing them monthly with four year cumulations of certain of them. The indexes are COM produced and printed.

Current telephone directories on microfiche, sold as *Phonefiche,* is a soundly conceived micropublishing enterprise that could save 95% of the space taken up by directories in major libraries. Most areas of USA and Canada are included as are key districts in other countries. The *Urbandoc Microfile* is on microfiche with a printed index and it covers urban planning and management; a useful library aid in dealing with local authority publications. *The Coordinated Occupational Information Network* is a multimedia publication offering school leavers and college students information on employment and educational opportunities in the United States. There is a micro-computer option that is not an alternative to the 90 microfiches but an enhancement of them.

35 mm microfilm, silver halide, archival standard, film is offered with the option of non-silver at considerably lower price, so that the librarian has to assess current usage against the archival needs of the library service. This company supplies positive non-silver vesicular microfiches. If negative copies are required diazo microfiches are supplied, but silver halide archival microfiches, positive or negative can be supplied. The normal reduction ratio is 24:1.

Bell & Howell is an equipment manufacturer and supplier and their being also a micropublisher should ensure their knowledge of and attention to the special needs of the library market. The fact that Micromedia Division carries out filming and silver duplication of 16 mm and 35 mm film and microfiche for several British and European micropublishers is also an indication of professional standing.

Chadwyck-Healey Ltd., 20 Newmarket Road, Cambridge CB5 8DT

Chadwyck-Healey Ltd are producing microform editions, not only of previously published material, but also of previously unpublished compilations. Such material is quite likely to be uneconomic to publish in any other way; it is also likely to be of considerable interest for research. *The Archives of British & American Publishers* is such a series. Chadwyck-Healey's list covers the subject areas of art, architecture, design, literary history and mass communication, political, social and local history, Official Publications and Official Statistical Serials.

It will be readily appreciated that major libraries will already have in stock sets such as *House of Commons Parliamentary Papers*, but, in addition to gap filling, total replacement of bound paper copies by microfiche will need to be considered by librarians because of rapid deterioration of the originals. There is also the matter of completeness to be considered, for the resources of major Government libraries are being exploited in order to make this microfiche series more complete than any existing set elsewhere. The *House of Commons Parliamentary Papers* on microfiche cover the periods 1801–1900, 1901–1921 and each session from 1975 to date.

An aid in the area of 'difficult' library material is *Catalogue of British Official Publications not Published by HMSO*, 1980 to date. There are bi-monthly issues and annual cumulations to this indexing service and it has the advantage of a microfiche on demand facility for the supply of full-text copies of any listed document required by a subscriber. This publisher offers individual works such as *The Diary of Beatrice Webb, 1873–1943*, on microfiche and data compilations such as *European Official Statistical Series on Microfiche*, and *British Government Publications containing Statistics, 1801–1977*. The wealth of material in the Library of Congress is tapped for such compilations as: *The Sanborn Fire Insurance Maps, 1867–1950* (623 000 maps of 10 000 American towns and cities reproduced on microfilm), *National Inventory of Documentary Sources in the United States* (registers of 772 collections in the Manuscript Division, Library of Congress, published on microfiche) and *Government Organization Manuals, 1900–1980*, (relating to the structure, organization and personnel of Government in 73 countries).

Archival quality microfilm is used and the publisher guarantees that the safety film stock conforms to ANSI standards, that it is free from 'hypo', that microfiche boxes and envelopes are free from harmful chemicals. Microform copies found to be physically substandard in any way will be replaced free of charge. In the USA Chadwyck-Healey Inc. operates from 623, Martenese Avenue, Teaneck, N.J. 07666.

Congressional Information Service Inc., 4520 East-West Highway, Bethesda, MD. 20814, USA

CIS publishes major microfiche collections of retrospective and current United States government documents, formerly published by several other organisations. They are valuable source material for academic, government, commercial and industrial libraries. Large orders attract free microfiche storage cabinets and readers. Only three of the series published by CIS are on microfilm (35 mm), all the rest are on microfiche. Only three of the microfiche series are diazo. The rest are silver halide, the majority negative polarity and between 18:1 to 24:1 reduction, with three series between 12:1 and 18:1 reduction.

The Federal Register's newspaper-like format in the original makes it difficult to store and preserve and thus the microfiche edition is a great boon to the reference librarian. The full collection of the *Code of Federal Regulations* comprises more than 3000 volumes so there is great space economy involved in stocking the microfiche edition. The *Congressional Record* is the 'Hansard' of the US Congress and so the archival silver halide microfiche edition is requisite for academic libraries. Other CIS publications include *Decennial Census Returns, American Statistics Index:* a comprehensive guide to the statistical publications of the US Government, *CIS Periodicals on Microfiche, US Supreme Court Records & Briefs* and, *Index to International Statistics* and its related microfiche library of the vast majority of the statistical publications referred to in the *Index*.

In Britain, Eire and West Germany, Thompson Henry Ltd., London Road, Sunningdale, Berks. SL5 DEP are agents for CIS micropublications.

Emmett Microform, 57a Lion Lane, Haslemere, Surrey GU27 1JT

The policy of this lively young company is to provide high quality colour reproductions of collections of drawings, photographs, artefacts and other objects in areas where there is very great need for this material. To date, their specialisation has been in fields of applied art, fashion and design which have been neglected in the past and which are the subject of present day interest and research.

Emmett Microform have concentrated on colour microfiche which is ideal, even necessary, for much visual material. Much of what they publish would be prohibitively expensive in printed book form with coloured plates and therefore probably would not be published. The microfiches are produced to an 84 frame format with some at 60 frames. Emmett Microform are the only micropublishers to include eye legible date and name frames within the fiche and this is obviously an added aid to easy use, although it adds to the cost.

Because they are selling colour reproductions, Emmett Microform have always concerned themselves with the quality of the reading equipment that the purchaser proposes to use, emphasising the need for good equipment, preferably screenless front projection viewers. Free advice on purchase and maintenance is offered. This firm promotes its micropublications in a market wider than that provided by libraries and recommends viewing equipment such as the Fuji RFP3 that enables group viewing and also projection downwards on to a sheet of paper, enabling students to trace. Thus they see the microfiche publication as not only a book photographically printed, but also a resource that can create material for students to use in project and other practical work.

The micropublications are supplied in heavy duty binders enabling their convenient shelving among the bookstock, if so desired. The allocation of International Standard Book Numbers should ensure the listing of these useful micropublications in the standard bibliographies. The publisher's list is attractively produced, in colour, with attention to good design. It is in an A5 folder of loose inserts each promoting a different series. In listing a selection of the published titles it is worthy of note that, the managing director being a qualified librarian, there is adequate provision of indexes to what is supplied. Titles include: *Visual Catalogue of Fashion and Costume in the Victoria & Albert Museum*, (over 4500 illustrations on 57 fiches of 84 frame format, together with an index of designers, engravers etc. Photographed in colour except where the originals are uncoloured); *Visual Catalogue of Miniature Paintings in the Victoria & Albert Museum*, (2300 miniatures photographically reproduced in colour on microfiche); *Theatre Costume Design in the Victoria & Albert Museum* (there are nearly 200 artists from 1589 to the present day, with a computer produced catalogue); *Paquin Worth, Fashion Drawings, 1865–1956*, (5000 designs on colour microfiche) and *Wallpapers, 1913–1941, Collected by the Silver Studio*. (24 fiches, 84 frame format, with 2000 colour illustrations).

Fashion Update is a colour microfiche serial published twice yearly after the spring and autumn fashion shows each year. *International Index of Design* is to be their first non-colour microfiche publication. Compiled by the Art & Design Library, Leicester Polytechnic, it is published annually. Emmett Microform's agents in USA are Somerset House, 417 Maitland Avenue, Teaneck, N.J. 07666.

Greenwood Press: a division of Congressional Information Service Inc., 88 Post Road West, Westport CT 06881, USA

The Greenwood Press microform catalogue divides its publications into two categories: Periodicals and Research Collections. The Congressional Information Service now directly publishes Government documents in microform that formerly were published by Greenwood Press. The collections are carefully selected, with printed bibliographies and indexes or other finding aids provided for each collection. The catalogue groups the periodicals into series such as: Nineteenth Century Children's Periodicals, Sports Periodicals and Science Fiction Periodicals.

The Research Collections are grouped as Playbills, AFL-CIO

Pamphlets and Plantation Records, for example. There is an interesting and potentially valuable *Urban Documents Microfiche Collection* which comprises American and Canadian local government publications over the last eleven years, on microfiche, together with a printed paper *Index to Current Urban Documents*. There are various subscription options. 24 160 documents were filmed to the end of volume 11 (1982–83), on 45 160 microfiches with 200 libraries and other agencies participating.

The microforms conform to the standards established by the American National Standards Institute and the former National Micrographics Association. The microfiches are positive silver halide, 105 mm × 148 mm carrying a maximum of 98 pages of documents and are at a reduction ratio of approximately 24:1. Microfilm is 35 mm positive silver halide roll film.

Thompson Henry Ltd., London Road, Sunningdale, Berks, SL5 0EP are the English agents.

Harvester Press Microform Publications Ltd., 17 Ship Street, Brighton, W. Sussex BN1 1AD

Micropublishers have a central role in making widely available the archival material in government and other repositories and libraries. In most cases microform publication is the only economically viable format. Whilst, in the past, librarians have encouraged scholars to visit their libraries to study unique collections and have been slow to agree to microform publication, more recently pressures on space, cost of staffing and shortage of funds have fostered consideration of the possibility of gaining income from micropublishing royalties. There has thus been a rich field of choice for micropublishing activities. This has encouraged specialisation in micropublishers' lists.

Harvester Press Microform Publications has two major specialisations, in British history and in music manuscripts. They attempt to build a comprehensive list of British history in their various microform programmes. This extensive list ranges from the *Episcopal Registers* of 1215 through to *Pressure Group Material* of 1983 and *Common Market Debate Sources*. No university or other institution of higher education can safely afford to ignore the Harvester Microform list. Selected series titles are: *The Central Records of British Government, 1547–1975; Complete British State Papers Domestic, 1547–1782*; and *The Politics and History of Modern Britain, 1770–1976. Music Manuscripts from the Great English Collections* is a facsimile microform edition of five great music collections, those of the Bodleian Library, Oxford, St.

Michael's College, Tenbury, Christ Church, Oxford, the British Library and the Royal College of Music, London.

35 mm silver halide, positive, archivally permanent, safety-base roll microfilm stock to ANSI standards is used, produced to NMA standards. There is a defective film replacement guarantee. There is concentration by this micropublisher on making available in microform some of the more important manuscript and other collections in the great British and European libraries to enable scholars to consult these documents in their own libraries — this is Harvester's policy rather than out of print journals or other re-issue micropublishing.

Inter Documentation Company A.G., I.D.C. Poststrasse 14, 6300, Zug, Switzerland.

Founded in 1957 in Tumba (Sweden) by Mr. H. L. de Mink, I.D.C. has had more than twenty-five years of rapid development. The processing plant is in Holland at Leiden and the company has always worked on the correct assumption that librarians would prefer their rare books, serials and manuscripts not to leave their own buildings. It has, therefore, mobile camera units in Leiden, Birmingham, Oxford, London, Tübingen, Munich, Boston, Washington, Mexico City, Jerusalem, Helsinki, Zurich and Vienna. There are plans, also, for New Delhi and Tokyo.

I.D.C. knows that users prefer microfiches to microfilm and publishes in this format with the exception of large runs of newspapers which it issues on 35 mm microfilm. Apart from user preference, this concentration on microfiche has made it economically viable to present the purchaser of sets above a certain selling price (S. Fr. 7500), with a free portable microfiche reader, (a choice of Realist Executive or Fuji RFP2). This has the great advantage that what is on offer is a research collection every bit as ready to read as if it were in book format.

The I.D.C. catalogues are excellent productions — illustrated and annotated. Additionally, there is advice on storage of microforms that includes allowance for tropical or air conditioned habitats. Silver halide archival standard film stock is used, positive, with 60 or 98 frames at reduction ratios between 14 and 20 depending on the size of the original works and the size of the type face in them. I.D.C. is experimenting with the production of colour microfiches with a longer life than those of other manufacturers, for use in art, historical and botany projects.

I.D.C. has over 600 000 volumes of monographs, serials, manuscript collections, archival collections, periodicals and newspapers available in microform. Subject fields covered are: agriculture, archaeology, architecture, art, African studies, Arabic studies, Asian studies, biology, botany, economics, government publications, history, history of science, Jewish studies, law, Latin American studies, languages and linguistics, literature, Middle East studies, political science, religion, Russia, East European studies, sociology, statistics and zoology. Examples of more recent projects are the *Fawcett Library Collection on Women's Studies, Amnesty International Archive Collection, Emblem Books* and the *Methodist Missionary Society Archives* as well as the independent Polish trade union publications of *Solidarity*.

Irish Microforms Ltd., 93b Sandymount Road, Dublin 4, Eire

Specialising in Irish archival material, this Company's catalogue lists over 20 titles on microfiche as well as more than 50 titles on 35 mm microfilm. Subject areas include Irish history, politics, literature and genealogy (including Griffiths Valuation). It offers backfiles of national and provincial newspapers from 1735 to date. In co-operation with various repositories in the country, manuscripts not currently available in microform can be commissioned through Irish Microforms Ltd.

All micropublications are produced on archival quality silver halide film to international standards. The microfiches are COSATI A1 105 mm × 148 mm, 98 pages per fiche at a reduction ratio of × 24, and COSATI A2 with 60 pages per fiche at a reduction ratio of × 16 is used where it is more suited to the original format. The reel microfilm is in 35 mm standard 100 ft reels in cine mode. 16 mm is used for special items as it allows better quality reproduction. Microfiche binders are supplied where a micropublication is in more than 30 fiches. The prices would appear to work out at about £16 per reel for microfilm and £1.70 per fiche.

The catalogue is available without charge. Microform publisher's catalogues are a useful source of more information than can be carried in the general bibliographies of microform.

Mansell Publishing Ltd., 6, All Saints Street, London N1 9RL

Mansell Publishing Ltd. are publishers of a broad range of bibliographic and other reference works. Their list includes publications in microform, but all are in one catalogue sensibly treated, with as full annotations as the printed books, together with ISBNs. The format is microfiche produced to NMA standards although there is one item listed as being on 35 mm microfilm and that, too, has a printed paper introduction and an ISBN. Listing in and retrieval from standard bibliographical sources is thus facilitated.

Original publications include, *Archives of British Men of Science*. This is claimed to be the first original microfiche publication in Great Britain. It locates unpublished material of some 3500 British scientists who flourished between 1870 and 1950. Another is *Sources for the History of the British in the Middle East, 1800–1978:* a catalogue of the private papers collection in the Middle East Centre, St. Antony's College, Oxford. Both these titles are on 60 frame microfiche whilst the others have 98 frames. An important title published in 1983 is *Proclamations, Broadsides, Ballads and Poems: The Halliwell-Phillipps Collection in Chetham's Library Manchester* on seven reels of 35 mm microfilm. Other titles include: *A Comparative History of Metrology*; Charles H. Cotter's *Studies in Maritime History*, and *British Policy in Asia: India Office Papers*. The practice has been adopted of reprinting in microform early parts of a series that have become out of print. An example is *ISIS Cumulative Bibliography, 1913–65*, where Volumes 1 and 2 were reprinted on microfiche in 1983, whereas subsequent volumes are available in print on paper.

The pricing of Mansell microfiches works out at between £2 and £3 each for publications involving one or two microfiches and £2 and under for those with higher numbers. In the U.S.A. and Canada, Mansell titles are available from the H.W. Wilson Company.

Microforms International Marketing Corporation, Fairview Park, Elmsford, N.Y., 10523, USA

MIMC is a subsidiary of Pergamon Press. In addition to the 346 Pergamon journals available in microform, the output of other micropublishers is listed in the annual catalogue and promoted. The pricing scheme is interesting and has the added attraction of the 1984 prices being held at the 1983 levels except in a few instances.

A subscription to the microfiche edition of a current journal can be taken out at 80% of the printed paper-rate. If microfiche is chosen it will be airmailed immediately after publication of the printed issue. If microfilm is chosen it will be sent immediately after the publication of the last issue of the year. Microform and printed editions together, to which one would subscribe in order to save all binding costs, are 150% of the printed paper price. There is choice of positive or negative, magazine or cartridge, 35 mm or 16 mm, or microfiche.

Back issues of all journals are available and out of print Pergamon books, as are new Pergamon Press micropublications such as *The Glasgow Edition of the Works and Correspondence of Adam Smith*.

Recently MIMC has concluded an agreement whereby a number of important *Oxford University Press* journals are being micro-published by MIMC on 16 mm and 35 mm microfilm and on micro-fiche from their first issues until the last volume published.

Microforms International Marketing Corporation's Catalogue, *Microforms Annual*, now in its 6th edition 1984/85, is distributed freely to libraries. Its 670 pages are divided into three parts: *Scholarly Serial Publications, Special Microform Projects* and *Current Serials and Related Microforms*.

Microform Ltd., East Ardsley, Wakefield, West Yorkshire WF3 2AT

This company, formerly trading as E.P. Microform Ltd., operates a uniform price policy by charging £25 per reel for silver halide microfilm, £2 per silver halide microfiche and £1.50 per diazo microfiche. Additionally, special pre-publication prices for certain larger new series are arranged. Microform Ltd., does not issue a complete catalogue under one cover, but a series of informative sectional catalogues. The main subject areas covered are: American studies, African studies, literature, fine arts, history, politics, social studies and church and missionary history.

The subject areas African studies and American studies include government publications, annual reports, blue books, statistical compilations, etc. The church and missionary history collections include key 19th century religious journals such as *The Church Army Gazette, 1888–1914* and *The War Cry, 1879–1939*. The art collections include: *The Illuminated Books Engravings and Water Colour Drawings of William Blake; The Paintings and Drawings of Dante Gabriel Rossetti in Public and Private Collections in Great Britain*, and *The Drawings and Water Colours of J. M. W. Turner, R. A*. The stated policy of Microform Ltd., is a willingness to learn from librarians and others of subject areas in which primary source materials, compilations, etc, are needed but are not readily available. Wherever possible a specialist in that subject area is then appointed as editor to ensure that academic control is maintained. Usually, an introductory essay, indexes and finding aids are provided in booklet form to a microform series.

Microfilm is the main medium with some microfiche availability. Electrostatic prints are available on demand of individual frames of these microforms and a search fee may be charged, as appropriate. Microform Ltd, also provide a contract microfilming service for manuscripts and other library materials, journals and newspapers.

Currently they are exploring video format options for their list.

Mindata Microform Systems, Wrexham Lodge, The Green, London W5 5EN

Mindata specialises in micropublication in the visual arts. With one exception the output comprises unique publications of material never before reproduced; the collections are indexed. Microfiche, supplied in binders, as preferred by librarians, is the chosen format. Both colour and monochrome microfiches conform to international standards and the latter are silver-halide duplicates of archival quality. Several series in the Mindata list are, however, produced on 35 mm microfilm.

The richness of this visual arts coverage is best conveyed by a selective list. Titles include: *A Photographic Record of the Wallace Collection; Fine Art & Design in the Victoria & Albert Museum; British War Art of the 20th century; Historical Prints in the British Museum; A Photographic Record of the Principal Items in the Collection of the Victoria & Albert Museum; Early Alinari Photographic Archives: Art and Architecture in Italy* and *Christie's Pictorial Archive*. A new venture is a picture research collection with reference material in microform, some half a million pictures with reproduction quality prints available on demand — *The Visual Arts Library*.

Mindata also distribute *Bibliothèque Nationale: Collections of the Department of Prints and Photographs* on 35 mm silver halide microfilm.

Ormonde Publishing Ltd, 76 Clancarty Road, London SW6 3AA

Although Ormonde are by no means confined to fine art micropublishing, pride of place must be given to their colour microfiche set, *The National Collection of Watercolours in the Victoria & Albert Museum*. This comprehensive collection of British watercolours, 1580–1980, only a few of which are on display in the museum at any one time, is thus exhibited in full on microfiche, in faithful colour, fully indexed both by each fiche carrying an index to its contents and by a complete set index on fiche.

Eighty-four frame format is used and this enables all paintings, whether landscape or portrait orientation to be viewed without changing the position of the fiche in the holder. Reduction ratios are between 17 × and 24 ×. The brochure is beautifully illustrated with pictures in the collection. It is hard to see how any art library can manage without this set.

Other art collections from Ormonde include *Leonardo da Vinci from the Royal Collection at Windsor Castle*, said to be the world's finest collection of his drawings. They are reproduced on colour microfiche with some black-and-white, some ultra-violet and some infra-red images. Also available are *Architectural Drawings in the Victoria and Albert Museum* on microfiche, *The Drawings of Raphael at the Ashmolean Museum* on colour microfiche and *Index to the Tate Gallery Archives*, on microfiche. In fields other than visual arts there are *Prompt Books* and *Actors' Copies of Plays in the Theatre Museum at the Victoria & Albert Museum* on microfiche and *The Library Catalogue of the Institution of Mechanical Engineers* on microfiche.

In the USA, Ormonde Publishing Ltd.'s distributors are Somerset House, 417 Maitland Avenue, Teaneck, N.J. 07666.

Oxford   Microform   Publications   Ltd,   The   Old   Malthouse, 19a Paradise Street, Oxford OX1 1LD

This company is a leading British micropublisher. A subsidiary company, Oxford Microform and Publishing Services Ltd., was formed in 1980 to enable copyright owners to choose their own preferred method of micropublishing. The first option is the usual arrangement, with OMP acting as licensee, bearing all the expenses, carrying out all activities and paying a royalty on sales. Should the copyright owner have publishing skills, then OMP Services Ltd., can supply just the additional expertise required. This requirement will be production only in some cases, but with the advantage of not just using a general bureau but an experienced micropublishing company understanding the entire process.

Another option is co-publishing or partnership. In this case the 'on-demand' and often specialist aspects of micropublishing are taken care of by OMP, whilst the copyright owner uses appropriate skills on a joint venture basis. This last arrangement works particularly well with, for example, Oxford University Press in respect of their major reference titles such as the *Oxford English Dictionary* and the *Dictionary of National Biography*.

OMP publishes collections of sources in various subjects that are of great value to academic libraries. Examples of these are: *Major Treasures in the Bodleian Library; Major Thematic Selections from Oxford Sources – Bestiaries – Apocalypses – Herbals; The Non-Fictional Works of H. G. Wells*, (71 titles, the collection in Bromley Public Library) and *Catalogues Compiled by the Contemporary Scientific Archives Centre*, Oxford.

An example of a previously unpublished work is H. W. Buxton's

History of Computing: a Memoir of the Life of Charles Babbage, (an 1871 manuscript in facsimile on 13 microfiches). Unless otherwise stated, publication is on microfiche. The microfiches are archivally permanent silver halide, positive, 98 frame, 24 reduction.

The fiche-book format is employed by this company for *ABSEES*, as well as for other publications. *ABSEES: Abstracts and Bibliography for Soviet and East European Studies*, would be unlikely to be viable published in any other way.

Back issues of journals available from OMP include *New Society* and *New Scientist* on microfiche (35 mm film is also available). Current subscriptions to the simultaneous microfiche edition of either journal are met by weekly mailing of microfiche which is of particular benefit to overseas readers. The *Journal of the London Society*, 1912 to date, is available on microfiche from OMP.

Oxford Microforms Publications Ltd., is now owned by Pergamon Press. It has been integrated with Microforms International Marketing Corporation with the intention of extending micropublishing activities both in Oxford and in New York.

Pergamon Press Ltd, Headington Hill Hall, Oxford OX3 0BW
See Microform International Marketing Corporation above.

Research Publications Ltd, PO Box 45, Reading RG1 8HF

When *The Times* Newspapers were sold to News International Ltd, the microfilming operation, Newspaper Archive Developments Ltd, remained with the International Thomson Organisation, PLC. Having originally been formed in 1972 to handle the production and marketing of *The Times Index* and microfilm editions of the various *Times* newspapers, Newspaper Archive Developments Ltd, was merged with Research Publications Inc, in 1982.

The catalogue indicates the major categories of micropublication as (a) newspapers and periodicals and (b) academic collections. The long established printed indexes are listed and continue to be available separately. The microfilm, unless otherwise stated, is positive 35 mm open reel polyester-based silver emulsion of archival quality to ISO specification.

The major production is *The Times* from the beginning in 1785, to date at 15 times reduction. Film of current issues is supplied monthly. The norm is positive, but negative can be supplied at 25% more. Related titles are: *The Sunday Times*, 1822 to date; *The Times Literary Supplement*, 1902 to date; *The Times Educational Supplement*, 1910 to date and *The Times Higher Education Supple-*

ment, 1971 to date. There is a discount on subscriptions for these micropublications if taken jointly with *The Times*. *The Times Literary Supplement* is available on microfiche. Other newspaper titles available on microfilm include *The Financial Times, The Sunday Telegraph, The Daily Telegraph, Lloyds List, The Scotsman, Illustrated London News* and *Le Monde*.

The academic collections available include: *The Eighteenth Century:* a microfilm collection based on the Eighteenth Century Short Title Catalogue containing 'every notable item printed in any language in Great Britain and its colonies, and those printed in English anywhere in the world between 1701 and 1800'; *The London Directories From The Guildhall Library, 1677–1855; Early American Medical Imprints, 1668–1820* and *City Directories of the United States of America*. Additionally, there are one or two collections on microfiche such as *Wall Street's Corporate and Industry Research Reports*.

The USA address is Research Publications Inc, 12 Lunar Drive, Woodbridge, Connecticut 06525.

K.G. Saur Verlag KG, Postfach 711009, 8000 München 71, W. Germany

The London address of this firm is K.G. Saur Ltd, Shropshire House, 2-20 Capper Street, London WC1E 6JA. Their microform catalogue stresses the improvements that have taken place from the 1970s to date. These comprise improvements in the design and construction of microform reading equipment making it usable in daylight and the general adoption of microfiche now successfully reproducing black and white half tones as well as colour.

K.G. Saur have concentrated on very extensive works or works which exist only as scattered fragments, such as the *Proceedings of the German Bundestag and Bundesrat*; genealogical handbooks such as *Gotha*, and the *National Collection of Watercolours*, on colour microfiches, which are easier to produce in microform, and, having a low economic production run, facilitates republication. Silver halide microfiches are the norm, but some titles are offered, alternatively, in diazo. *Gesamtverzeichnis des Deutschsprachigen Schrifttums* (Bibliography of German language publications 1911–1965) is available in microfiche edition (390 fiches) with choice of silver or diazo.

Interestingly an ISBN is given for each of Saur's micropublications, which should be general practice. As with certain other micropublishers, some material listed is not published by Saur, but distributed by them, but these titles are clearly indicated.

Universitetsforlaget, Microfilm Division, PO Box 2959, Toyen, Oslo 6, Norway

This Norwegian Universities joint publisher commenced microfilming operations in 1981 with a commitment to microfiche for the micropublication of Norwegian governmental and parliamentary papers.

University Microfilms International, 30-32 Mortimer Street, London W1N 7RA

University Microfilms International produces its film and fiche in the USA, on demand, as required to meet orders. The micropublications are priced in dollars and 3% has to be added to listed prices for shipping and handling charges. An enormous and ever-growing archive of master film that was started in 1941 enables this to be done; hence the size of the list and also the preponderance of film over fiche in what is on offer. This is what one would expect from the pioneer micropublisher, but I imagine that a gradual change over to microfiche will occur.

There has been change over the years in the business organization itself. University Microfilms International is now represented in Europe, the Middle East, Africa and Australasia by Information Publications International Ltd at the above address, and in South East Asia and the Far East by Information Publications Pte Ltd, Pei-Fu Industrial Building, 24 New Industrial Road, 02-06 Singapore, 1953. The USA address continues to be U.M.I. 300 North Zeeb Road, Ann Arbor, Michigan 48106.

The latest U.M.I. catalogue of journals, periodicals and newspapers is *Serials in Microform, 1983*. This is a paper bound reference work giving full bibliographical details, availability of current and backfile years and pricing for each of the 13 000 titles it contains. Entries also indicate whether the original publisher has produced an index and in which commercial indexes the title is cited. Entries are arranged in alphabetical order according to the Anglo-American Cataloguing Rules. A subject index is also included. Most titles are available in 16 mm or 35 mm film or microfiche. *Serials in Microform, 1983* is itself also available on microfiche, very sensibly as it runs to some 900 pages.

Over 700 000 doctoral dissertations are available from U.M.I. in microform with the alternative option of buying as xerographic reprints. Several subject catalogues of dissertations are produced each month, updating the list of the 30 000 new titles added every year. As these catalogues are selective, being a form of current awareness promotion, the enquirer can search the active listing by title via U.M.I.'s *Datrix II* computer or via Lockhead *Dialog*. They are, of course, the entries that appear in *Dissertation Abstracts International*.

U.M.I. has passed the 100 000 mark in acquiring reprinting rights to out-of-print or rare books. All titles are listed in a new cumulative catalogue — *Author Guide, 1983*. Each entry gives full bibliographic details, including author, title, imprint, edition, series, volume and price. This catalogue is also available on microfiche. Between November 1980 and September 1982 6761 titles were added to the *Books on Demand* programme and these are listed in a supplement *New Titles, 1981–1982*. Items listed in *Books on Demand* are available either in microform or xerographically reproduced.

Research Collections in Microform, 1982 lists over 40 research collections. New projects are very clearly indicated. *American Presidential Election Campaign Biographies, 1824–1972* is an example. This has 465 titles on 1367 microfiches at US $1955 with a free printed index, together with William Miles's bibliography, *The Image Makers*. Catalogue entries have been fed into the OCLC database and customers not having access to OCLC can acquire catalogue cards via U.M.I. The simple expedient of U.M.I. joining OCLC will ensure future savings in cataloguing to OCLC member libraries when they buy U.M.I. collections.

U.M.I. now has the *New York Times* in microform in its list, (35 mm microform). There is twice monthly delivery on subscription. Back files are available 1851 to date. The edited weekly microfiche version is available back to 1981 only. The *Index to the New York Times* is available in printed and bound format. The subject coverage of U.M.I.'s list is so wide that one tends to look there first when checking on availability.

All U.M.I. microforms are produced on high quality polyester-based silver halide film of archival standard. It is guaranteed to comply with ANSI PH 1:41(1976). They state that advanced ageing tests show that when stored in recommended conditions, 70°F (21°C), or lower, with relative humidity 30–50% U.M.I. microforms will last for centuries. The major output is 35 mm film but there is a growing availability of microfiche.

Having the world's largest and most comprehensive selection of serial publications in microform U.M.I. has begun to cater for current users with no interest in archival quality. Where this meets one's needs, the current year, only, can be purchased on non-silver stock at 15% less. Other features of U.M.I.'s service include a serials subscription service and an article copying service.

The serials subscription service provides for a single invoice for current paper issues followed by the microform version as soon as it is available. The article copying service provides on demand prints of articles from titles in U.M.I.'s serials in microform collection at a standard charge where the rights to do so have been acquired, as indicated in the serials catalogue.

University of Chicago Press Ltd, 5801 Ellis Avenue, Chicago, Illinois 60637, USA

The current approach of this publisher is called *text-fiche* and it comprises short-run printing of texts coupled with numerous microfiche illustrations. This has led to the development of a list of 44 art publications with the text in conventional format and illustrations photographed on colour or black-and-white microfiche. Publications include catalogues of museum holdings and archives and catalogues raisonnés of artists' works. These publications are additional to University of Chicago Press books and they are promoted and listed with their ordinary publications.

The London address of The University of Chicago Press is 126 Buckingham Palace Road, London SW11 9SD

University of Toronto Press, University of Toronto, Toronto, Canada M5S 1A6

In 1971 the University of Toronto Press began issuing its new titles on microfiche at the same time as they appeared in regular book form. This far sighted pioneer enterprise deserved much more success than it achieved. Considerable attention was attracted to the scheme, but the level of orders that was essential to its success did not materialise. This remained the case even when the marketing of simultaneous microfiche editions was turned over to an established micropublisher.

In an article in *Scholarly Publishing* in 1975, Ian Montagnes indicated that behind the decision to publish in this way was the conviction that the potential value of microfiche for academic publishing needed to be demonstrated by a university press for purposes of 'consciousness raising' and for gaining actual experience of micropublishing. The aims of the University of Toronto Press in this respect were fully achieved[1].

Ease of access, second only to the book, with ability to locate instantly any chapter or page, were seen to be the reason for the popularity and potential of the microfiche format. The trend to tighter library budgets then beginning, it was felt, would accelerate the adoption of microforms for space saving reasons. Known reader resistance and the inadequacy of bibliographic controls which hinder access to micropublications were not allowed to prejudice the enterprise. As the microfiche copies were seen as extra run-on copies of the printed edition of a book, the simultaneous publication policy involved the same list price for print on paper and microfiche as, also, did the need to produce royalties for authors. There was, however, a later experiment in marketing which allowed 40% discount if one bought both editions, an arrangement that did not increase the sale of the microform editions.

In spite of its financially unrewarding pioneer experiment in micropublication, the University of Toronto Press did not cease to micropublish, although it did give up simultaneous publication of full sized and microform editions. Titles that are so substantial as to make publication in print impracticable appear on microfiche. An example is *The Complete Diaries, in holograph and typewritten transcription, of the late W. L. Mackenzie King, Prime Minister of Canada*. This publication comprises 223 silver halide microfiches and a printed chronological index covering the period 1893–1931. There is more of this valuable source material of modern Canadian history to follow.

Another type of micropublication from this university press is represented by *Candide*, being a computer generated concordance on 9 microfiches housed in the back of a printed paper study of the work. Another is *Canadian Books in Print*, which is a quarterly, on diazo microfiche because the publication is updated and therefore the microform does not need to be of archival quality. The University of Toronto Press licenses others to produce microform back issues of its journals.

World Microfilms Publications Ltd, 62, Queen's Grove, London NW8 6ER

This company produced its first microforms in 1969, but it also publishes books, journals and audio-visual materials such as tape-slide series, slides and audio cassettes. However, 70% of the company's annual sales are microforms. World Microfilms Publications Ltd specialises in colour microfilms of illuminated manuscripts. Its subject coverage is in areas of great interest to an academic readership in art, mediaeval history and literature, the cinema and architectural studies. An example is the *Royal Institute of British Architects' Drawings Collection* on microfilm.

Shakespeare in Context is a compilation on microfilm of source material relating to Shakespeare's life, time and works. It is in five parts each prefaced by a detailed, scholarly introduction and bibliography on the microfilm with a separate printed index. The parts are Prologue: the life; Shakespeare's theatre; the social and intellectual context; Shakespeare's sources and the texts. 35 mm roll film is used but microfiche can be supplied. Similar 'context' series are planned, surely an ideal application of the microform medium, bringing together out-of-print and new material of diverse formats with specially prepared introductions, indexes and specialist bibliographies.

I am conscious that listing items from a micropublisher's catalogue can be misleading because of the very selectiveness that limitation of space involves, but a brief indication can only be helpful. World Microfilms Publications offers *The Winchester Bible and the Winchester Cathedral Manuscript Collection; The Papers of the South Sea Company, 1711–1856; The Russia Company: Minute Books and Treasurer's Accounts, 1667–1955; The Visitation Returns from the Dioceses of Canterbury and London, 18th–19th Centuries* and *Trinity College, Cambridge: the Mediaeval Manuscript Collection.*

Reference

1. MONTAGNES, I., "Microfiche and the scholarly publisher", *Scholarly Publishing*, October (1975) pp 63–84.

Suggestion for Further Reading

Microform Review, Volume I 1972 to date. The review sections for micropublications of interest in stock-building.

Five

Library catalogues: COM and on-line

Developments in cataloguing

Until just recently, one major area of professionalism in libraries was cataloguing. It follows that the required result of the professional librarian's expertise was a full catalogue of the library's holdings, completely up to date and as accurate as human frailty would allow. In many libraries this was often achieved to a very high degree. Where this was not the case, sometimes due to bad management, or where amalgamations into larger systems, or rapid growth, produced large backlogs, there was pressure to automate.

Of course, some libraries with very good catalogues wished to modernise their techniques, in any case. In the early days of the general adoption of computers for administrative tasks, surplus capacity indicated to librarians in the local authorities and the universities the possibility of using the computer to produce and maintain their catalogues.

This initial phase of automation in libraries, based, as it was, on assisting the public authority or other institution to justify high expenditure on its main-frame computer by providing an additional use for which it was not primarily designed, did not produce the best results. In the area of cataloguing it resulted in poorer service to library users, involving, perhaps, use of a card catalogue for older books and a microform catalogue for current additions whatever their date of publication.

Ultimately it resulted in standardised entries in all types of library catalogue and the relegation of much of the work of the local cataloguer into clerical routine. The establishment of the British National Bibliography in 1950 was a landmark on this road to centralised computerised cataloguing.

The British National Bibliography

From the outset the British National Bibliography was conceived to have three functions that are still appropriate to a national biblio-

graphy today[1]. These arc:
1. to constitute a current awareness tool from which to select stock;
2. to provide a cumulative bibliographical reference system for retrospective literature searches;
3. to provide a vehicle for centralised cataloguing with all the potential economies that that involves.

In addition to weekly issues based upon the copyright deposit of books by British publishers, there are monthly index cumulations and quarterly, annual and five-yearly full cumulations. There is also the catalogue *card* service. Clearly, like the Library of Congress in America, the British National Bibliography has provided considerable encouragement for standardisation.

Because of the volume of data handled, both these services rely heavily upon computer facilities. Thus the BNB, which is now the responsibility of the British Library, Bibliographic Services Division, receives machine readable catalogue input from the Library of Congress, which, in its turn, receives machine readable BNB input. Neither country need catalogue the publications of the other and centralised cataloguing has progressed from a national to an international basis. It was thus the obvious next step to provide access to the BNB and Library of Congress machine readable catalogue records (MARC), to support computer based catalogue schemes in those individual library services that wished to subscribe. Before looking to these more recent developments, however, we should take some note of the earlier pioneering efforts.

Pioneers

First in the field were the public library systems of Camden, Greenwich and Barnet, all in the London area, which already had computer-produced paper print-out catalogues by the time that Westminster City Libraries started planning its computerised catalogue system in 1967. Larkworthy[2] recounts that when Westminster's computer-produced catalogue was ready to start production in 1970, no available output system could be found that was cheaper than the expensive computer print-out on to paper, photocopied to produce the additional sets required. However, later that same year, computer output microfilm became available in the UK and so a COM bureau was approached and a trial film of the computer catalogue file was produced.

It was observed that the public appeared to have no problems in operating the hand-wound cassette reader used during the trial period and so readers of this type were adopted when the COM catalogue system was put into full service. The new catalogue medium effected a very great saving in cost per catalogue, although, of course, there were extra costs involved in acquiring the COM readers. Also, in due course, the comparatively cheap hand-wound readers gave way to more expensive motorised reading machines.

Other British pioneers, together with Westminster City Libraries, were Cornwall County Libraries, West Sussex County Libraries, Cheshire County Libraries and the London and South East Region Union Catalogue (LASER). In the industrial library field, Imperial Chemical Industries, Mond Division and Unilever Research Ltd., led the way with COM catalogues.

Encouraged by the availability of grants from the Office of Scientific and Technical Information of the Department of Education and Science, computerised catalogue schemes for individual university and public libraries were started with the aim of achieving goals that were more likely to be met on a realistically economical basis by centralised national or regional services[3]. These and similar services, possibly of local application only in some instances, tended to provide less catalogue information than is normally considered desirable. This was perhaps because the emphasis was on finding an acceptable system suited to local needs in cases where the existing centralised scheme appeared to be too detailed, even pedantic, in meeting the known local library user approach. With hindsight one can see that what was needed was a full national system with facilities to draw from it just the level of detail required for each application.

The computer output microform catalogue systems in certain university libraries quite consciously sought to avoid the complexities of the full entries on the MARC file and adopted shortened entries. The development phase of these systems was well documented for the benefit of other libraries[4]. In the matter of very short entries, it is interesting to note that one of these libraries later added author's initials in order to enhance the usefulness of a very approximate finding tool.

MARC-based schemes

Computer-based library catalogue services that are likely to be viable in the longer term are firmly based on the British Library/ Library of Congress MARC data base. This includes the co-operative cataloguing schemes such as BLCMP, SCOLCAP, and SWALCAP, described below, as well as those systems that merely use the MARC base without co-operating with other libraries. Output from these systems can be in any computer output microformat, such as microfiche or cassetted film, or, indeed, on-line. Of these, the most likely at the present time is computer output microfiche, although there are some libraries still utilising cassetted roll-film.

Cassetted roll-film had earlier been chosen as most readily maintaining 'file integrity' in view of the large file size involved in a library catalogue. Libraries opting for microfiche, however, demonstrated that the problem was largely imaginary, for microfiche are generally neither misplaced nor stolen. The apparent convenience of cassette format library catalogues with 100 ft (30 m) of film feeding from one completely enclosed reel to the other was halved when the manufacturers pointed out that although 100 ft could be carried, best results were achieved with only 50 ft[5]. Cartridges, on the other hand, house only one spool and need a specially designed take-up spool on the machine.

On-line remains the choice of very few libraries, because of the costs involved. The libraries of the Universities of Sussex, Reading and Bath and The Polytechnic of the South Bank each have some part of their catalogues available on-line for their readers' use. The City University has an on-line file of recent additions, books on order, and books in process, in one sequence, for staff use, with computer output microfiche main catalogue.

Computer output microfiche catalogues are cost effective and monthly up-dating is normally adequate. It is usual to provide consultation points throughout the library additional to those in the catalogue area. An actual example of capacity is a full catalogue of 110 000 records on 144 microfiches with a short entry catalogue on 20 microfiches. It is usual to employ the services of a COM bureau to convert the local library tape or disc to the required microphotographic format. These bureaux are highly competitive and more than one quotation should be sought.

BLAISE/LOCAS

As to the actual preparation of local library input to a computerised cataloguing data base, old routines cannot be adapted. Instead, a systems approach to what the required output should be involves rethinking the whole cataloguing process. This done and appropriate procedures adopted, then the use of a centralised service such as British Library/LOCAS involves the subscribing library in quoting the ISBNs, or, where this is not possible, the Library of Congress numbers for the books to be added to stock together with the accession number or numbers, location indicators, headings and other data such as local variant classification.

These details are added to the LOCAS MARC record for that library service. For additions to bookstock that do not have either an ISBN or Library of Congress number or for which such cannot then be discovered, specially planned data input forms are completed. These present the information in a way that is MARC compatible. Either the forms themselves or tapes keyboarded from them may be sent in to BLAISE by subscribers to the LOCAS scheme.

The MARC tapes are then searched for the records required and some are not found. Some libraries have decided that it is too time consuming to continue to resubmit those not found and they catalogue these themselves. In the matter of timeliness in the cataloguer finding entries for his current accessions in the national bibliography, the adoption of the *Cataloguing in Publication* scheme represents a not entirely successful attempt to obviate criticism about time lags between publication and appearance of details of that publication in the national bibliography. In a scheme such as *Single Stream* LOCAS, if a *Cataloguing in Publication* entry is selected, the library is forever left with that imperfect entry for it is not updated automatically to the corrected entry. Where a library is part of a co-operative scheme such as the *Union* LOCAS of London University, then corrected entries for one library update those for all member libraries.

The British Library Automated Information service, which operates from The British Library, 2 Sheraton Street, London W1V 4BH, had, as of December 1983, eighty-three customer libraries for its Local Catalogue Service (LOCAS). These were public, academic and special libraries in the United Kingdom and Eire, plus two overseas customers. About half of these are members of the three co-operative schemes that BLAISE/LOCAS services, namely, SCOLCAP, University of London and the Inner London Education Authority. The scheme, introduced in August 1974, offers a complete cataloguing service from data preparation to catalogue output on a centralised basis. Those libraries with some in-house or local computer facilities can, if they so wish, subscribe to a modified service and receive COM tapes.

For each participating library, LOCAS maintains a local MARC-based catalogue file consisting of centrally produced UK and Library of Congress MARC records and locally created records for material which is not available from the British Library data base, (the data base is UK MARC, 1950 to date plus L. of C. MARC, 1968 to date). The file is processed monthly to produce an updated catalogue, normally on microfiche, although subject indexes and special listings can be produced on paper if preferred. The LOCAS served co-operatives we have mentioned have a shared union file whilst receiving catalogues relating to each individual library in the group.

A growing trend is for libraries to select records on-line from the central data base and to transfer copies into intelligent terminals which have their own storage facilities. These records can be edited and amended off-line, cutting the cost of computer connection time, before running the records to LOCAS.

BLCMP

The Birmingham Libraries Co-operative Mechanisation Project deserves pride of place in alternative schemes as the pioneer of 1969, becoming operational in 1972. It is a totally independent non-profit making company owned and directed by member libraries. There are 38 member libraries, including 8 public, 7 university and 16 polytechnic systems. The founding institutions were the Universities of Aston and Birmingham and Birmingham City Libraries, making use of the MARC data base for centralised co-operative cataloguing and adding entries for many foreign and older works not represented in MARC.

BLCMP offers both on-line and batch services, and maintains extremely large data bases on its own mainframe computer. A country-wide network of private telecommunications circuits provides access for all on-line users into BLCMP's central computers. Stand-alone and shared systems are operated, with planned development of a comprehensive range of library applications in both modes, including public access to on-line catalogues. The address of BLCMP Ltd., is Main Library, University of Birmingham, Birmingham B15 2TT.

The data bases include all BNB cataloguing, post 1950, together with Library of Congress, post 1972, and all BLCMP participating libraries own extra-MARC input. There is an acquisitions system on a shared system basis, later to be available as a stand-alone option and a full circulation control system available in stand-alone mode. Charges are on a once only basis at point of entry for each record. Microfiche is by far the most frequently chosen output format for catalogues.

SCOLCAP

The development of the Scottish Libraries Co-operative Automation Project began in 1973 and soon became grant-aided by the British Library. The primary objective has always been a fully on-line network to provide a system for acquisitions, cataloguing, information retrieval and the provision of library management statistics.

The first achievement, as elsewhere, has been the successful implementation of an off-line cataloguing system using BLAISE/ LOCAS services on a co-operative basis. The seventeen co-operating libraries receive computer output microfiche catalogues, and, in some cases, output on magnetic tape as well, to facilitate automated internal housekeeping routines such as circulation. A co-operative data base of in excess of 775 000 entries, was by late 1983 being made available on-line to member libraries.

With initial equipment funded by the Scottish Education Department, the on-line system is based on a dedicated mini-computer linked to BLAISE and made accessible to libraries via leased lines and intelligent terminals, of which 96 can be simultaneously accommodated on-line. The mini-computer holds a core data base satisfying the majority of requirements while the link to BLAISE provides on-line access to the total MARC file. Thus, if a record is not available on the SCOLCAP data base, the switch to BLAISE is made automatically. SCOLCAP operates from the National Library of Scotland, 312-320 Lawnmarket, Edinburgh EH1 2PJ.

SWALCAP

The South West Academic Libraries Co-operative Automation Project, based on the Bristol University Library was set up in 1969. It first developed a circulation system by 1976, a cataloguing system by 1978 and later a computerised book ordering system. It is an on-line service used by some 20 libraries, each having its own file. Records for each system are supplied by other members or BLCMP or BLAISE.

The issue system involves terminals in member libraries linked by leased lines on-line to the SWALCAP computer. The local library terminals can operate independently off-line as necessary.

GEAC

GEAC is a Canadian system now extended to Europe. The claim is made that it offers a complete service for every library requirement now and in the future. These needs are circulation, cataloguing, acquisitions and statistical information; all available as an integrated system or as individual options.

The University of Hull Library and The Polytechnic of the South Bank are users. The UK address is GEAC Computers Ltd, 1690 Park Avenue, Aztec West Almondsbury, Bristol BS12 4RA.

ORIEL

ORIEL Computer Services of 1-5 West Street, Chipping Norton, Oxon OX7 5BR, have been supplying library cataloguing and circulation control systems in Europe, (particularly Holland), since 1972.

These were largely batch run systems, but now an on-line system is offered using Sirius microcomputers. Oriel's first British installation was the Metropolitan Borough of Wirral Libraries, in 1983.

OCLC

OCLC, Europe, operates from Lloyds Bank Chambers, 75 Edmund Street, Birmingham B3 3HA. On-line accessing of the OCLC 9.4 million MARC record data base, it is claimed will provide in excess of 90% of a library's needs. The matched records can then be loaded into local systems, both stand-alone and shared.

Local charge dialed access is offered with a £30 per hour connect charge and the records are supplied on magnetic tape.

Conversion of existing catalogues

Bearing in mind that it is probable that catalogues in printed and bound book format are the most acceptable as far as library users are concerned and that it is equally apparent that sheaf catalogues have always been considered the next best thing, the card catalogue coming a poor third in the user evaluation list, the librarian should not rush into partial solutions to problems.

Conversion of existing library catalogues involves careful consideration of all the problems and proposed solutions, the cost of all present and proposed cataloguing operations — capital as well as recurrent costs — and seeking to select the option that best serves the readers at reasonable cost. It is well to bear in mind that whatever reader preference might be, catalogues in printed book format have not been economically viable this century and that sheaf and card catalogues being labour intensive are now too expensive to maintain properly. Also relevant are the findings of a survey by the University of Bath Library to the effect that 69.9% of users disliked the card catalogue, 19.2% disliked roll film, 9.6% disliked microfiche and 1.3% disliked computer print-out[6].

The advantage of retrospective conversion of catalogues is the achievement of a unitary format machine-readable catalogue data base for a particular library service. Then, whether the present choice of output format be microfiche (for economy) or on-line, the future position is safeguarded by the existence of a growing machine-readable file. There would, of course, be little merit, other than space-saving, in microfilming the retrospective catalogue for use in the intervening time until it can be added to either a computer output microfiche or an on-line system.

If an existing card or sheaf catalogue is retained and closed it from a given date, changing over to computer-based cataloguing for all new accessions and amendments, there is a need to ensure that the cataloguing staff have a programme of checking a required number of the old entries against the shelves and against the computerised catalogue each week and feeding them into the new system. A catalogue closed from a given date without such a phasing-out programme, long-term though it might need to be, rapidly becomes forgotten. Becoming little used it continues to take up space whilst the books it lists are not used.

The advent of REMARC has made even the conversion of large catalogues of past accessions easy, but not cheap. REMARC is the retrospective conversion of all non-MARC catalogue records of the Library of Congress. Charging to libraries is based on the 'hits' or the records successfully matched against the data base. These are then added to a library's own data base.

The finding rate is likely to be high because L. of C. has the largest stock in the world. REMARC data base is a product of Carrollton Press Inc, of Arlington, Virginia, USA. Chadwyck-Healey Ltd, of Cambridge is the agent for UK and Europe for off-line supply of records.

For libraries of national importance, with appropriate resources, computer *input* microfilm is being used to cope with the conversion of monumental existing catalogues such as that of the British Library Reference Division. The British Library has access to the Department of Health & Social Security GRAFIX I CIM machine at Newcastle. Optical character recognition is used, but, even so, much expensive preparation is essential[7].

Benefits of computer-based systems

As has been noted above, in order to gain maximum advantage from a computerised system, one can set up a file that carries entries for books from the time of their ordering. The status of each title can then be recorded through receipt and accessioning to its being catalogued and taken into use.

There is economy in staff time in checking requests for new additions on-line to the library's own mini-computer. The one-sequence check on the VDU obviates the need for searching, interfiling and retrieving from order card indexes as well as a main catalogue sequence. The automatic recording of books issued on loan, recall and overdue notice production, issue statistics, etc., are all facilitated. All types of library stock can be included in one set of records with ability to produce selective listings for special purposes.

At this stage it would be most unwise to attempt to design a computerised system for a specific library operation from scratch; one should utilise an existing service, centralised, co-operative or both[8].

The choice of an existing system may involve total adoption or application in part, but selection must be based upon a careful survey of the longer-term needs of the particular library. Equipment selected must be compatible with existing and planned future equipment on the road to a total 'housekeeping' system. Better still, it should be adaptable to possible electronic library developments. The nature of present day information technology equipment, however, involves a five year programme of amortisation and, thereafter, replacement by the next generation of equipment.

References

1. WELLS, A. J., 'The British National Bibliography, 1950–1974' *Cat. Index*, 34, 7–10 (1974).
2. Proceedings of a COM cataloguing workshop seminar, 8 November, 1972, NRCd Occas. Pap. No. 6, 68 pp. (2 microfiches) (1973)
3. BUCKLE, D., 'The use of computers in university libraries for housekeeping purposes', 53 pp., private circulation, SCONUL (1973)
4. University of Bath, Bath University Comparative Catalogue Study, Final Report, Bath Univ. Library, 10 papers, various paging (1974–76)
5. HADLOW, J. F., 'Some problems with COM catalogues'. *Microdoc*, 16 75–82 (1977)
6. CAUGHLIN, C. 'BUCCS Seminar Report', *Cat. Index*, 36, 7, 10–11 (1975)
7. CLEMENTS, D. W. G. 'Conversion of the General Catalogue of Printed Books to machine readable form', *J. Librarianship*, 15, 3, 206–213 (1983)
8. HAWES, D. F. W. and BOTTEN, D. A. *Library automation at the Polytechnic of the South Bank*. Library Association (1983)

Suggestions for Further Reading

1. BAKEWELL, K. G. B., 'Cataloguing and classification', in *British Librarianship and Information Work, 1976–1980*, ed. L. J. Taylor. Volume 2, ch. 17. The Library Association (1983)
2. TEDD, L. 'Computers and networks' In *British Librarianship and Information Work, 1976–1980*, ed. L. J. Taylor. Volume 2, ch. 19. The Library Association (1983)

Six

Data services

General

Data services are central to the move toward the electronic library. Just as periodical publications were the first category of library stock to become generally available in microform, so abstracting and indexing services were the first to become generally available as computerised on-line services.

In each of these categories there were very good reasons for the move to non-print formats. The chief of these reasons were the availability of the newer medium with its need to find a larger market and the suitability of the newer medium for the purpose in hand. Data services, too, are clearly the leaders in the use of the newer information technologies of computerised retrieval from microform and from optical digital disc.

Prestel and Teletext are digital data carrying systems that are familiar in our libraries. These are discussed in chapter 8.

The vast existing store and ever growing volume of the literature of science and technology, world-wide, has led, in the past, to attempts being made to produce compilations of data, abstracts and indexes centrally. Waddington, writing in 1967, saw co-operative effort as the way forward because, 'the day of the coverage of all science by a single centralised editorial effort has passed. The problem has become too large for any one group.'[1] Further it precludes the possibility of any one abstracting service covering a unitary subject, such as chemistry, in its totality, without the participation of subject experts in each country. Thus the trend to ever more specialised abstracting services continues, although it is likely that clues to the resolution of present day enigmas in one field of learning are increasingly 'revealed by the serendipitous juxtaposition of bits of knowledge not thought of as connected'[2].

It is relevant to consider what the data base is and to look at the so-called 'information explosion'. The volume of literature appears to go on growing and much writing, particularly in the field of scientific information, has implied that here is an eternal growth situation. However, explosions terminate and the information explosion looks to be more of a temporarily self-perpetuating effervescence of twentieth century vintage. Much information is continually repackaged and recycled.

It must be admitted that many papers are published mainly for academic advancement. Lest that sounds too cynical one must hasten to add that whatever we call it, the data base constitutes the finding medium for the key seminal and subsequent developmental papers on matters of great continuing importance to mankind, as well as the dross. Sound professional librarianship involves providing access to all of it without evaluative bias.

No serious research in any subject can safely proceed without a careful literature search to discover what has already been written on the topic. De Solla Price, in a publication of 1963, stated that an estimated 10% of the research and development budget of the USA was spent on inadvertently duplicated research[3]. This percentage, almost certainly, will have been greatly reduced by improved abstracting and indexing services and library training in literature searching techniques in the intervening years.

It is now generally agreed that sound information management involves the *author* of an article in writing an abstract or very brief précis of its subject content. Depending on the particular needs of the subject, the abstract may be either indicative or evaluative. In either case an abstract is best written by the author as the person most able to determine what the writing is about.

Of course, it remains true that certain major abstracting services employ professional experts to prepare their abstracts. When published, the article plus the abstract is a piece of primary publication. The abstract adopted by an abstracting service, indexed (by author, subject, title, keywords in or out of context, formulae, etc as appropriate) and made available in printed, micrographic, electronic or other form is a secondary publication.

Sold almost entirely to libraries, abstracting services commenced in printed format. Having evolved in the 1960's to using a computer in producing the publication, the next step was to make the computerised data available to subscribers, first in computer output microform, then as a computerised service accessed in batch mode, then, later in the 1970s, on-line.

In using data services there are several questions to which one needs to know the answers with a considerable degree of certainty. These are

1. The stated coverage of the service, that is to say, for which journals does it carry abstracts, what other publications are included, is it world-wide or limited in coverage;
2. The degree to which its claimed coverage is effective;
3. The speed of updating;
4. Access to the service, that is how it is indexed;
5. Whether it is well indexed along the stated lines.

A data base composed of the range of indexes noted above together with full abstracts is very demanding on computer storage.

In printed paper format, services such as Chemical Abstracts are enormously space consuming on library shelves.

If we proceed to full text availability of the articles we will have, not a data *base* but a data *bank*. A library is such a data bank, and, at the first stage of development, bound printed paper abstracts and indexes are searched for references, the appropriate primary publications are retrieved from the shelves and read or possibly a photocopy is supplied.

The second stage of development can be represented by Dr. Atherton Seidell's then revolutionary proposal of 1934. Writing in *Science*, he put forward the idea of photographing the required articles, and mounting the photographs 'in windows in filing cards'[4]. Further, these aperture cards were to remove the need for expensive inter-loan systems by being sent off to the requesting library for retention.

Later, it became commonplace to use rapidly machine sortable code-punched aperture cards in information systems in industry and commerce. Although there were limited schemes in America involving the sending of strips of film in lieu of inter-lending, the possible inter-loan application has not found favour although it could remove both waiting lists and the cost of keeping inter-loan issue records. Copyright, together with the vested interests of national lending libraries are obstacles.

The third stage of development was batch access to the computer data base of the abstracting service. This can be via a licensee 'host' system or direct and can include SDI searches, that is to say matching terms submitted (a profile) as being a particular researcher's field of interest[5]. What is supplied, however, is the content of the data base only, that is abstracts.

The final stage of development that we will include here presents full-text retrieval via a variety of options. These full-text options obviously include the established pre-mechanisation procedure of checking the printed paper indexes and abstracts in the library and retrieving the article from the printed paper journal on the shelves of that library, which remains the most 'user-friendly' option. Normal library usage, however becomes greatly less 'user-friendly' when the item required proves not to be on the library shelf and the frustration and expense of seeking to borrow it commence.

Other options include searching abstracts and indexes either in printed paper format, in microform or on-line and receiving the full text either in print-out or in microform or displayed on the VDU. The VDU full-text can originate either on-line, or via facsimile transmission or locally from a microcomputer-aided retrieval device selecting the appropriate microfiche frame. The full text storage held centrally can be either microfiche on automated retrieval machines or video disc; it is less likely to be on magnetic tape or magnetic disc.

Specimen abstracting services

A brief examination of two major abstracting and indexing services will be indicative of what is offered by these services in general.

Chemical Abstracts is a joint venture by The American Chemical Society and the Royal Society of Chemistry. The basic content, is Chemical Abstracts, 1907 to date; specialised sub-sections also being available. The whole range of formats is on offer; printed paper, microfilm in cassette, microfiche, magnetic tape and on-line, but the coverage on-line by the end of 1983 went back only to 1967.

Considerable price benefit is offered to the purchaser of the printed edition over the microfilm or microfiche price. The reason seems to be the false assumption that purchase of a microform edition implies a desire to indulge in extensive copying, thus reducing the demand for the original service.

As to the on-line service, whilst a special graphics terminal is needed for the display of chemical structures, any terminal can be used to access CAS on-line. This service can be used as an example to indicate the complicated charging methods typical of such systems. Firstly, there is a fee for setting up an account. Secondly, there is an hourly charge for connection on-line, there is the telecommunications usage charge and charges for current awareness and full-file searching. By providing instant access at speed to searching by chemical structure, substance names, title word or phrase, author, researcher, inventor, institution, keywords, trade names, ring data, molecular structure etc, *Chemical Abstracts Service* on-line displays the additional benefits such services can provide over older retrieval procedures.

INSPEC provides indexing and abstracting in the physics and engineering disciplines and is a major venture of the Institution of Electrical Engineers. It is typical in that it publishes a data base users' guide, a thesaurus of terms used, a guide to its classification system and a list of journals abstracted. Abstracts journals are available in printed paper format, in microform with film and fiche options, and on-line. *INSPEC* is typical in not supplying copies of the original papers indexed. It displays the general trend to specialisation with new on-line services such as *Electronics Materials Infor-*

mation Service. It has a magnetic tape service which is designed for organisations operating their own computer-based information systems. *INSPEC* on-line is available via *Lockheed Information Systems, Data-Star Marketing* and *European Space Agency Information Retrieval Service* among others.

On-line now

In considering exactly what a computer search achieves, it is important to note what it does not do. Normally, at the present time, it does not provide a copy of the full text of the article selected, but only a full text of the abstract. Many services do provide the facility of being able to order a copy of the full text for a further charge.

In many services the data base covers the more recent years only. Computer data base searching saves time and usually provides a more thorough and more complex search. It provides lists of references and abstracts where they exist. A small but growing number of data services are available as computerised services only; that is to say, there is no printed version.

Full text retrieval will increasingly be offered by purveyors of the small data bases. *Harvard Business Review* began to be offered on-line during 1983. The full text availability, however, was back to 1976 and only a bibliographic base with abstracts from 1971. The full text data base is, of course, being expanded retrospectively.

Agencies

Imperfect, incomplete, yet overlapping coverage of subjects by different abstracting services on separate data bases has encouraged the development of agencies that carry more than one service. These are sometimes known as Information Documentation Centres and they acquire leases to make other people's machine-readable files available to customers. First this tended to be in batch mode and then later on-line.

A library can act as such an agency. The Science Reference Library Computer Search Service offers *CA Search, World Patents Index, Medline, Compendex, Scisearch, Biosis, INSPEC*, and *Promt*. Examples of agencies on a commercial basis are *DIANE* and *DIALOG*.

DIANE, the Direct Information Access Network for Europe is the EEC's commercial centre for information using thirty-five host computers to provide access to 300 data bases. *EURONET* is a data transmission network especially set up for international on-line information with retrieval at cheap rates via the various PTT authorities. *DIALOG* provides a variety of subject coverage with more than 150 data bases carrying in excess of 55 million records in science, technology, business, economics and social subjects. It has a facility for searching the various data bases sequentially. Full text can be ordered on-line at extra charge for subsequent mailing.

Information on data services

Since 1979 there has been an On-Line Information Centre supported by the Department of Industry and the British Library Research and Development Department, housed at ASLIB. A listing of UK on-line publishers with addresses, appeared in the *International Journal of Micrographics & Video Technology*, Volume 2(4), 1983, with an addendum in Volume 3(2), 1984[6].

Perhaps the most useful source of information, however, is *Encyclopaedia of Information Systems and Services*; 5th edition published by Gale Research Company in 1982. This carried 2522 entries and the first periodic supplement, entitled *New Information Systems and Services*, July 1983, listed more than 330 new ones in detail. An examination of this useful publication indicates rapid growth with increasing specialisation of on-line information services.

Simultaneously there is also a trend to mass appeal information services that can be accessed by users in their homes and public libraries using microcomputers or videotext. This directory gives information on both types of service.

The future

Information provision by the early 1980s had developed into a vast and increasingly profitable industry. This irrefutable economic fact was responsible for certain readily apparent trends.

First, there is the readiness of the private sector to mount attacks attacks on the public providers of information for so doing, if not freely, then at cost, thus providing 'unfair' competition to the private sector. Thus the US National Library of Medicine was under attack by *Excerpta Medica*, an Elsevier subsidiary, for its provision of *Index Medicus* and leasing MEDLARS/MEDLINE data base tapes to agencies at disputed 'full cost recovery' charges.

Secondly the role of the librarian came to be under attack. One very useful business information on-line service advertised in the following terms: 'Information retrieval is speeded up with more precise and thorough powers of recall. It saves money and *replaces librarian style information storage . . . and filing arrangements that use expensive staff time. (Textline.* Finsbury Data Services Ltd, London). The *Financial Times New Media Markets Newsletter*, Volume 1(2), carried a note 'developments . . . combining SDI and text searching techniques of the many data base systems with electronic mail and news alerting services to almost any type of terminal, word-processor or telex, *looks as if it might at long last break the stranglehold of the librarian on the market for electronic business publishing'*, and then comes the throw-away sentence: 'It is seen as a breakthrough to levels of management *able to spend far larger sums on information'.*

The question to be dispassionately answered is, will such new technology services make the librarian redundant? The answer is 'certainly not', but it does serve to remind us of the need for readily evaluated service from committed professionals and an explicit philosophy of librarianship.

Increasing sophistication of computer capability will increase the flow of data services into libraries. More does not necessarily mean better and more informed librarianship in utilising funds to the best service of readers is necessary. I refer here to purchase of new equipment and the type of services and not to the information which they carry. Take-up of information services has not been rapid. From the first hesitant steps into using scientific and technological services on-line, librarians have progressed to regular usage of services such as *Eurolex* and *Lexis* in the field of law. All such services involve additional costs and if the customer library pays for a few references by using selective services rather than by purchasing an entire abstracts journal, then, since the overheads still have to be paid, the price per reference has to rise.

On-line services having grown as a side-line to the production of abstracting and indexing services, the use of the same computer tape for the production of a printed publication and for on-line information retrieval represented a bonus to the publisher. There is now a need to produce computer tapes where the emphasis is on ease of retrieval rather than storage.

Interaction between the user and the data base via an intelligent microcomputer in the library is the next step. This involves a total systems approach from a pre-publication point. Nevertheless, there are problems about this; not least there are trade union problems, for the obvious reason that increased automation means fewer jobs. One can cite difficulties such as that in Fleet Street, where, I believe, print unions now allow journalists to produce their work directly on word processors but require it to be output thereafter in a typed format from which the compositors set up the type using their own keyboards. We are some way from the once only keyboarding of an author's manuscript together with its abstract that will be the basis for composition and printing and for secondary publication and for all the machine readable bibliographical recording, abstracting and indexing entries that will enable inter-active retrieval.

References

1 WADDINGTON, G., 'A world system of evaluated numerical data for science and technology' *J. Chem. Doc.* 7, (Feb. 1967) pp. 20–23.
2 SHEPHARD, F. C., 'The various roles of secondary publications (some thoughts)' *Int. J. of Micrographics & Video Technology.* 2, 2 (1983) pp. 101–104
3 PRICE, D. J. DE SOLLA, *Little science, big science*, Columbia University Press (1963)
4 SEIDELL, A., 'The photographic reproduction of documents', **Science** 80, (1934) pp. 184–185
5 LUHN, H. P., 'A business intelligence system' *IBM J. Res. Dev.*, 2, (1958) pp. 314–319
6 POWELL, D. 'UK On-line publishers' *Int. J. Micrographics & Video Technology*, 2, 4 (1983) pp. 269–280 and 3, 2.

Suggestions for Further Reading

1 MASTRODDI, F. and LUSTAC, S. 'EURONET DIANE: a precursor to electronic publishing?' in *The future of the printed word*: the impact and the implications of the new communications technology; ed Philip Hills. Francis Pinter Ltd (1980) pp. 111-121.
2 KING, J. *Searching international data bases*. 174 pp. British Library (1983)
3 HOOVER, R. E. ed *On-line search strategies*. Knowledge Industry Publications Inc., (1982)

Seven

Copying from non-book media

The law of copyright

Copying is subject to restrictions imposed by the Copyright Acts and Regulations in force. The origins of the law of copyright are to be found in the natural desire of human beings to protect their own property — in this case intellectual property. Additionally there are elements of state censorship and monopoly in the history of copyright protection. The Stationers' Company, in recording a publication in their Register, were granting a perpetual right to a property, and this right could then be inherited.

The state's interest in requiring publications to be entered at Stationers' Hall lay in achieving a measure of censorship to prevent sedition, and publications were thus effectively licensed. Modern British copyright law began with the Copyright Act of 1709, which enacted protection for fourteen years for new publications and a term of twenty-one years for any in print at the time of the enactment. These works, already in print, had previously enjoyed perpetual protection. At the end of the twenty-one years, large-scale reprinting of the now unprotected works started. This limited, rather than perpetual, ownership of intellectual property was established as a privilege granted by statute rather than as a presumed common law right.

Copyright law in the USA has its origins in an Act of 1790. Subsequent case law parallels English law in the adoption of the concept that copyright ownership is really not a property right stemming from common law but rather a privilege granted through government enactments which enunciate the principle and then designate the term of protection allowed[1]. The US Copyright Acts of 1790, 1831 and 1870 were superseded by that of 1909. Between 1955 and 1976 revision was under active study, all interested bodies being busy putting conflicting viewpoints, but the issue was much complicated by the availability of technology that enabled comparatively easy full-sized reprography, micrographic, computer and computer plus microform replication of copyright material.

The need to safeguard the interests of authors, publishers, librarians, library users and educationalists delayed the presentation of a new Bill. President Ford signed a bill for a general revision of the United States copyright law in October 1976. This became a statute in force from 1 January 1978.

The UK law of copyright is undoubtedly most confusing to the layman. The Copyright Act of 1956 (ch. 74, 4 and 5, Elizabeth II), protects all literary material for a period of fifty years from the end of the year of first publication of the work, or fifty years from the death of the author, whichever is the later in time. New editions of works out of copyright are protected for twenty-five years from the end of the year of publication of that edition. The protection includes restriction of acts such as reproducing the work *in any material form*, or publishing it.

Section 15(1) of the Copyright Act of 1911 remained unrepealed by the Copyright Act of 1956. This section of the 1911 Act relates to the deposit of published books at the British Museum Library (now British Library, Reference Division) and other national copyright deposit libraries. Opaque microforms, it can be held, are subsumed by the term 'books', as that expressly includes single sheets of letter-press, etc.

These copyright deposit requirements do not cover microfilm or fiche publications in any obvious way. The Copyright Act of 1956 also fails to make specific mention of microfilmed books and other documents, in spite of the fact that they had long been with us by this date. Of course, where copyright subsists in the book microfilmed, it also subsists in the microcopy version. Opaque microforms are given copyright protection by the 1956 Act as they can be held to be printed items in the normal sense and indeed are often examples of photolithographic printing[2].

As mentioned above, the copyright protection of the original extends to the authorised microcopy. Powell believes that Section 3(1) of the 1956 Act refers to photographs 'irrespective of artistic quality' and it is as such that the microfilms themselves are pro-tected and, further, that this interpretation is supported by the photographic section of the British Library's Reference Division. Powell goes on to add that 'in the United States the micropublisher is less fortunate than in the UK, for there is not the mention in US legislation of the words "irrespective of artistic quality" and the Copyright Office has in fact declined to accept a registration of a microfiche edition of some public domain documents'[3].

Fair copying

Sections 7 and 15 of the Copyright Act of 1956 and Statutory Instru-ment 1957, No. 868, specifically allow 'fair copying'. That is to say, they allow of copying which *prima facie* constitutes infringement, provided that certain conditions are met. These prescribed conditions clearly restrict 'fair copying' to parts (not the whole) of published literary works. Thus no copy may extend to more than one article in any one part of any one publication and no person may be furnished under the regulations with two or more copies of the same article.

'Fair use', as a concept that is regarded as an acceptable variation from enjoyment of full protection by the owner of the copyright, exists in UK copyright law but was not actually contained in a US statute until 1976. The new law added provision for recognising a 'fair use' limitation on the exclusive rights of copyright owners. In practice, of course, a considerable body of case law on fair use had grown up in America. Briefly, fair copying may be taken to be the ability freely to copy part of a copyright work for the purposes of research and private study. The amount copied, in all fairness to the author and publisher, should not be such that it could conceivably prejudice the sales of the original publication.

The (American) Joint Libraries Committee on Fair Use in Photo-copying Report of 1961 had the following conclusions[4]:

1 The making of a single copy by a library is a direct and natural extension of traditional library service.
2 Such service, employing modern copying methods, has become essential.
3 The present demand can be satisfied without inflicting measurable damage on publishers and copyright owners.
4 Improved copying processes will not materially affect the demand for single copy library duplication for research purposes.
5 The Committee recommends that it be library policy to fill an order for a single photocopy of *any published work* or part thereof.

The American librarians, in paragraph (1), were putting forward the view that having bought a copy of a book for the use of their readers it does not matter in what form the work is used (either in the original or copy). There must be factors of cost involved in addition to copyright in the case of copying whole works, however. Also, the cost of copying represents income not to the author and publisher, but only to the manufacturer or hirer of the photocopying facility.

In paragraph (3) the key word is 'measurable', for if whole works were copied from microforms financial damage to publishers and authors might be considerable without being readily measurable. Paragraph (4) is almost certainly true except in the category of new (that is, previously unpublished) material coming to libraries in microform. The demand for copies of this type of library material might well build up because of the presence of good cheap copying facilities.

The publishers disagree with the findings of the Joint Libraries Committee on Fair Use. A librarian having reservations about any of the points enumerated above would still believe that it should be permissible for a library to copy even a complete book if it cannot be obtained new by reasonable effort.

The Whitford Committee

During 1975, Mr. Justice Whitford's Committee was convened to review the law of copyright. Among others, the Microfilm Association of Great Britain prepared and submitted evidence to the committee, recommending that:

1   Because they differ substantially from printed books, because of their extensive use and the customary practices of copying from them, the transparent microtexts should be covered by explicit statements in copyright legislation.

2   The publisher of a microform edition or republication should qualify for protection of the format and graphic design which he introduces. This could be effected in clauses similar to those on typographic arrangements in Section 15 of the 1956 Act.

3   Limits should be set by legislation (or if necessary in subsequent regulations) so that copying without prior permission is restricted within the concept of fair-dealing. These limits should be adequate to protect against unfair copying from microforms, recognising that a major portion of a book or other document may be recorded as a very small proportion of the contents of the micropublication.

4   Section 15 of the Copyright Act, 1911, should be amended to require the deposit of published works, whatever may be the material or means of manufacture of the copies, provided that the availability of such copies has been such as to satisfy the reasonable requirements of the public, having regard to the nature of the work. Only original publication or first publication of a revised edition should be covered in this way, except where, because of the date or place of publication, the original work was not subject to deposit.

5   The arrangements for deposit of such publications in microform should be as follows:

(a) The publisher should be legally obliged to offer a copy to the British Library.

(b) The British Library, if requiring a copy, would be obliged to pay a sum based on the cost of materials, plus labour, plus direct overheads.

(c) The copy deposited should be of the best material in which the microform is produced.
(d) The British Library should notify the British National Bibliography of microforms which are offered to it under the proposed legislation.

In both the UK and the USA, then, there is an element of conflict of interest between on the one hand the authors and publishers and on the other the users of libraries and the makers of copying equipment.

In 1977 the Whitford Committee report was issued[5]. In the chapter relating to reprography, *blanket licensing* was proposed to cater for all user requirements for facsimile copies, including library, educational, government, industrial and professional copying. The report also stated that '. . . the new Act should make it clear that microcopies are simply facsimile copies and that the relevant provisions apply accordingly. It will be open to the parties involved to negotiate special terms and conditions for this category of copying if this is thought to be appropriate.' Again, paragraph 963 of the Summary of Recommendations states: 'It should be made clear in any new Copyright Act that micropublications which are not mere copies of earlier editions are protected as published editions.'

The Whitford Committee put forward the view that Section 15 of the 1911 Copyright Act (that is the section dealing with legal deposit) should be covered by separate legislation. In this connection the Committee specifically mentions 'the question of microform publications should be considered' . . . (and) . . . 'the question of relieving publishers from the financial burden involved in legal deposit, possibly through fiscal concession, should be considered'.

Williams & Wilkins Co case

In recent years the Williams & Wilkins Co case has drawn attention to the more or less universal library interpretation of 'fair use' in photocopying articles in learned journals. In 1968 the Williams & Wilkins Co, publishers of many learned journals, brought a case against the libraries of the National Institutes of Health and the National Library of Medicine for infringement of copyright.

The National Library of Medicine apparently adopted the procedure of microfilming articles in journals whenever a request was received from another library. A full-sized photocopy was then produced from the microfilm and sent to the requestor. This was done on a large scale but nevertheless resembles 'fair copying' in the UK and other countries. One cannot believe otherwise than that periodical publishers currently price their journals in full knowledge of the library market's needs and practices. In 1972, the trial judge found for Williams & Wilkins Co that none of the criteria of 'fair use' had been present in copying; it was found that the libraries had indulged in wholesale copying without regard to the purpose of the use, the nature of the copyright work, the amount copied in relation to the whole, or the effect of the copying on the sales of the original. It was stated that in 1970 the National Institutes of Health Library had met over 85 000 requests for photocopies of journal articles including journals published by Williams & Wilkins Co. The requests totalled about 930 000 pages or possibly 93 000 articles.

The US Government appealed against the decision and the Court of Claims reversed the decision on the grounds that loss of sales caused by unrestricted copying had not been proved. To this statement of non-demonstration of financial loss was added the point that in the interests of the advancement of science the copying could be considered desirable. The Supreme Court in December 1974 considered an appeal and could not reach a verdict! The vote was 4 for and 4 against.

The Williams & Wilkins Co. appears to have been as much concerned with a resolution of what the law actually was as with any deep concern for possible compensation for infringement. The new American law puts statutory limits to the length of extracts from copyrighted material that may be copied without charge and also the number of times per annum that such extracts may be copied. Microforms and the newer non-book media are clearly included:

'Copyright exists in original works of authorship fixed in any tangible medium of expression now known or later developed . . . from which they can be perceived, reproduced, or otherwise communicated, either directly or with the aid of a machine or device.'

American librarians have had their concept of 'fair use' under the terms of the new act challenged by publishers to the extent of legal action on several occasions since 1978.

Copyright clearance

There was much less worry about copyright in microforms when the material microcopied consisted largely of out-of-print, out-of-copyright material. Now that much new material is being published solely in microform, there is a new interest and urgency in resolving copyright problems. Micropublishers in dealing with copyright material have to acquire rights and licenses from the owners of the copyright. While a periodical might involve dealing with only one copyright owner, many other publications involve several owners of copyright. Also, some publishing houses can be difficult to trace. They may have gone into liquidation or been amalgamated with others in rather obscure ways. All these need following up on occasion as do heirs, executors and assigns.

Lack of space suitable for library expansion has, on occasion, caused librarians to be urged, by what might be called the 'film it and throw it away' school or the 'film it and sell the originals' school, to take steps towards miniaturisation of library stock by arbitrary microfilming. Blanket remedies to problems are usually unrealistic; the major problem is copyright. Of course, out-of-copyright, 'public domain' material *may* be microfilmed but it does not follow that it *should* be so filmed. Factors relating to the nature of use as to frequency and intensity, type of material, etc, should all be taken into account. Where published microform versions exist these should be acquired rather than resorting to having the filming done again. All material protected by copyright should be the subject of individual requests for permission to copy, which will probably not be forthcoming.

Copyright does matter and cannot be ignored. One or two industrial libraries in the USA have filmed in this way in the past, on the ground that they are using the film in place of the printed copies they have bought and discarded — *ergo*, the author and publisher are not harmed! The librarian of one such firm reputed to do this was careful to let me know that I was misinformed and, of course, he would not microfilm copyright material! Space had been saved by filming 'public domain' journals only.

Some teachers hold that it should not be necessary for them to write to the author and publisher to acquire clearance for even quite extensive copying of copyright materials to be re-issued in learning packages. Librarians, too, are committed to the concept of free exchange of information, but usually within the bounds of 'fair dealing'. One cannot accept that educationalists who want free and unlimited use of copyright material are unaware of the problems involved, for many of them will themselves be authors!

The declining cost of copying

In the past the cost of copying from microforms in libraries has been a very real deterrent to infringement of the copyright of micropublishers. The advent of plain paper machines able to produce copies at the press of a button is making copying from microforms as easy as xerographic copying of printed material.

All copying is a matter of concern to the librarian. When a few pages of a book are copied within the fair dealing provisions of the

Copyright Acts and Regulations, no harm is done to the author and publisher. However, given the growing availability of machines that can rapidly and cheaply copy complete microforms on to plain paper, then both author and micropublisher will suffer pecuniary loss. It has to be borne in mind that such loss is proportionately greater in low volume publications such as are most micropublications.

Copyright declaration

Generally speaking, librarians would not knowingly contravene the law of copyright by countenancing such copying, but others might. British law, at least, makes the librarian responsible for copying taking place in his or her library.

The librarian has the responsibility of ensuring that all types of copying machines have warning notices displayed in proximity to them. These should indicate that it is an offence to copy material that is protected by the Law and Regulations relating to copyright. Also there must be a request form for such copying which bears a declaration upon it that the copy is required for purposes of private study and research. This must be completed, signed and handed in before the copying is done and a charge for copying should be made.

An attitude of mind should be fostered among library staff that microforms are provided for use on microform reading machines and are not to be copied needlessly.

International copyright agreements

The Universal Copyright Convention provides protection on an international basis once a country is a signatory. There are some peculiarities, however. The catalogue of one American micropublisher states: 'Foreign works not copyrighted in the United States and exhibiting non-compliance with the Universal Copyright Convention's specific requirements are offered as public domain classification and sold only within the United States . . .'. This indicates the need for micropublishers to conform to the appropriate regulations in all their likely markets.

Many countries are signatories to both the Universal Copyright Convention and to the Berne Copyright Union. The former dates from 1952 and exists specifically to extend copyright control to states that, for various reasons, cannot accede to the Berne Convention. The protection under the Universal Copyright Convention stems from

1 that country's acceding to the Convention, and
2 the works to be protected bearing a copyright notice consisting of

an encircled c, thus ©, the name of the copyright owner and the year of first publication.

The Berne Copyright Union was set up in 1886 and is basically a union of countries undertaking reciprocal copyright protection to the publications of the other signatories. This is blanket coverage without separate registration and gives full protection just as if the publication originated in the host country.

Blanket licensing

The 1981 Green Paper on copyright reform reverted to the Whitford suggestion of *blanket licensing*[6]. It is difficult to see how blanket licensing could work. Much material copied from microforms would be out of copyright, so licensing the copying machines by total usage would be inequitable. A counting device on the copying machine operated by an opto-electronic identifier of material in copyright incorporated into the microform itself would be equally unjust in increasing the price level of the equipment. The US Copyright Office reported to Congress its views on the first five years of the operation of the Copyright Act. On balance, the publishers' viewpoint is endorsed, and non-statutory recommendations include collective 'licensing to copy' agreements, a surcharge on copying equipment, and payments to publishers based on sampling of the copying actually carried out in libraries.

In Sweden, the government pays a lump sum to a collecting agency, based on sampling of the actual volume of copying in return for schools being allowed multiple copying rights. Licensing agreements allowing libraries to copy will not be happily accepted anywhere, and, in any case, it is essential to avoid setting up a parasitic bureaucracy to administer such arrangements if copyright owners are to receive any worth-while benefit. Enforcing such licensing in practice must be very difficult.

A copyright licensing agency was set up in Britain in 1983 by the Publishers Association, the Periodical Publishers Association, the Association of Learned and Professional Society Publishers, the Society of Authors and the Writers Guild. Its aim is to collect fees for copying at the rate of 4 p. per page of a book and 10 p. per page of a periodical, plus a levy of £10 per copying machine. It is intended by the agency that the proceeds would go to publishers and authors, 50/50 in the case of books, but that all the income in the case of periodicals would go to the publishers. The astonishingly high level of charges proposed by the interested parties would, if implemented, prove self-defeating, for additional library funds would not be made available and so fewer books would be purchased.

Other non-book media

It is not only an author's written words that are protected, but also dramatic, musical, artistic works, photographs, films, sound and visual recordings and broadcasts. The rights of performers are not included under copyright law but are separately covered and are protected in Britain and certain other countries.

The Whitford Committee had evidence from interested parties to the effect that the 1956 Copyright Act fair dealing provisions should be extended to cover excerpts of sound recordings, films and broadcasts for educational purposes. In the USA jukebox owners pay an annual license fee and cable television operators (other than instructional cable systems) also pay a levy. The US Supreme Court early in 1984 ruled that home video recording from televised films does not constitute a violation of copyright law.

In West Germany there is a levy on tape recorders. The proceeds are distributed to agencies for the benefit of composers, performers, authors and record companies. Academic libraries in Britain commonly record off air on to video tapes, for purposes of private study and wipe the tapes within one year, within the concept of fair dealing.

Encouraged by the Government's Green Paper[6], Television Channel 4 has appointed an agent to operate on its behalf a pioneer recording licensing scheme that will allow educational and training establishments to record designated programmes off-air on to video cassette and use them for study and training. Fees are to be set according to the category of educational establishment and range from £1 per programme up to £20 per programme for twelve months use. One awaits the outcome with considerable interest!

The British film industry has, since 1950, been financially assisted by the levy of a sum added to the price of each cinema ticket. This income, used to help finance new films, dwindles as cinema attendances drop and currently the film industry is lobbying for a £1 levy on each sale of a blank video tape. Such a levy would, clearly, be unjust in that blank video tapes bought for *any* purpose, including education, would be taxed in order to finance the entertainment industry. If such a proposal were implemented, the way would be clear to extend it to cover the sale of blank audio tapes.

This matter is closely related to the problem of making copyright law effective, for film companies also sell their products on video tape and unlawful copying on to blank tapes undermines their market. However, it is the sale of unauthorised copies that is lucrative and it is at the point of sale that the existing law can be strictly enforced, thus making a levy on blank tapes unnecessary.

Case law in California holds that *software* in printed form, *on screen* or on *silicon chip* is protected by copyright. The US Registrar of Copyrights has drawn attention back to the fact that copyright law is only incidentally concerned with the physical artifact, being primarily interested in the work embodied in that artifact. Thus the new technology such as optical disc will have enormous impact in its ability to carry so much copyright information and at the same time facilitate its copying at remote terminals.

Some librarians might like to believe that the new technology, of its very nature, could make copyright law obsolete and allow all information to be provided free. Things will not happen in this way, indeed no commodity is free, and information will continue to be paid for in the future, probably by on-line electronic transfer of funds. The publishers' scheme ADONIS is discussed in chapter eight.

A new UK Copyright Act?

The time that has elapsed since the publication of the Government Green Paper[6] in July 1981, clearly signals that is is not official policy to enact a new Copyright Act as a matter of urgency. There have been private members' bills on aspects of copyright, without any chance of success or of influencing government towards a blanket enactment.

There is a feeling that existing legal provisions can be better enforced and that discrete aspects of increased copyright protection can be picked off one at a time. Thus, for example, unauthorised copying from video tapes and stealing computer software can be dealt with separately, avoiding the need for difficult governmental decisions.

The appropriate pressure groups such as the British Computer Society are busily promoting action on copyright materials, each in their own sphere of interest, whilst the British Copyright Council presses for a new all-embracing Copyright Act, so far without avail.

References

1 BEARD, J. J., 'The copyright issue', in *Annual Review of Information Science & Technology*, ed. C. A. Cuadra and A. W. Luke, Vol. 9, 381–411 American Society for Information Science, Washington (1974)
2 POWELL, D. J., 'The law of copyright in relation to publications on microfilm', *Microdoc*, 13, 34–37 (1974)
3 POWELL, D. J., Unpublished paper on copyright given at an MAGB Seminar, Edinburgh (1974)
4 Joint Libraries Committee on Fair Use in Photocopying. Report on single copies, *Bull, Copyright Soc. USA*, 9, 79–84 (1961)
5 Copyright and Designs Law: Report of the Committee to consider the Law on Copyright and Designs. Cmnd 6732, HMSO (1977)

6 Reform of the law relating to Copyright, Designs and Performers' Protection. A Consultative document. Cmnd 8302, HMSO (1981)

Suggestions for further reading

TAYLOR, L. J. *Copyright for Librarians*. 164 pp. Tamarisk Books (1980)
The ABC of Copyright. 73pp. Unesco, Paris. (1981) [Not an ABC in the usual sense but a brief booklet with useful chapters such as: 'Duration of protection', 'Copyright formalities', etc.]

Eight

Information technology and libraries

By information technology is meant the present day convergence of technologies that are useful and profitable in their own right to form together a powerful new approach to information storage, transfer and retrieval. These are the technologies of computers, telecommunications and micrographics with microelectronics as the facilitator. This process has aptly been described as 'synergistic combination', for the result of working together is much greater than the sum of the individual parts[1].

Today computer-assisted retrieval is commonplace, using systems that combine the above technologies. In this chapter consideration is given to the various electronic applications that are increasingly the carriers of information in libraries — electronic-micrographic, electronic-magnetic and electronic-video based systems. Far less noticeable to the library user than the new technology apparatus itself is the undoubted characteristic of information technology, that is, that the basis of paying for information is totally changed by it.

Traditional publishing is funded by a one-off payment on the purchase of a publication, but using modern electronic media involves payment on each consultation. The growth of information documentation centres where enterprising middlemen get the income from the results of the publishers' investment, has led to great interest being shown by the publishers themselves in electronic publishing. New technology, too, encourages the marketing of 'publications' in all the new media. Some categories of publication are seen by publishers as being capable of profitable marketing direct to the user, thus by-passing not only documentation centres (data base lessees), but also libraries.

The use of information retrieval equipment no longer requires any special understanding of computing techniques. Equipment is gradually becoming 'user friendly', with prompts coming up on the screen as to the next operating step and 'menus' of choices being displayed. Touch screens are the ultimate in user friendliness in removing even the need for ability to use a keyboard.

Information technology: an historical note

The following brief historical note seeks only to provide background information to those who do not have it. It lays no claim to be a history.

Computers

The abacus has aided man's basic arithmetic at least since 3000 BC. Simple machines using numbered wheels for computing addition and subtraction were built by Pascal in 1643, and Leibnitz in 1672. By 1812, Charles Babbage had the idea of calculating numerical tables by machinery; later he held the Chair of Mathematics at Cambridge and became a Fellow of the Royal Society at the age of 24[2]. A small Babbage machine was put together in 1820, but his design of 1835, although the machine was never constructed, led to his being regarded as the 'father' of the modern computer. Using punched cards, similar to those successfully used by Joseph Jacquard to control the pattern woven by a loom, Babbage conceived a memory store and a processor each controlled by its own punched card programme.

The succeeding innovators included Leonardo Torres who developed electro-mechanical computing with some programming, 1915; Vannevar Bush, who in 1931 designed a differential analyser (an analogue computer), and Douglas Hartree and Arthur Porter who made an analogue computer from Meccano parts in 1933. In 1936 Konrad Zuse pioneered basic concepts of automatic computing using the binary system and Claude Shannon and George Stibitz in 1937 evolved electrical switching circuits on Boolean principles. In 1944 the Harvard Mark I calculator was made.

It is customary to categorise computers proper into generations. The *first generation* used vacuum tubes and can be represented by ENIAC all-electronic computer (1946) and EDSAC (1949) which had a high-speed memory. The way was prepared for microelectronics by the 1948 invention of the transistor by Bardeen, Brattain and Shockley at Bell Laboratories; by the invention of the solid state amplifier in 1951 and by the achievement of semiconductor packages in 1959. The *second generation* computers of the 1960s used transistors as switches in central processing units but still had magnetic main core memories. In 1971 logic and arithmetic functions were first performed by a single tiny silicon chip, a microprocessor (INTEL), opening the way for future generations of computers. In 1975 the INTEL complete computer on a single printed circuit board was perfected. The *third generation* computers were thus much more compact, with integrated circuits on chips. The *fourth generation* computers, including microcomputers, utilise large-scale integrated circuits, many miniaturised on one micro-processor as a central processing unit. The *fifth generation* will com-press both the central processing unit and a large amount of high speed memory into very small compass.

Thus, microminiaturisation of components, economising on materials and power consumption, has already produced micro-computers capable of handling as much information as the massive early computers. They are commonplace in our homes and schools and a growing presence in libraries. By the mid-1980s they will have formidable interactive capabilities and will be a vital information resource.

Audio

Edison's 1877 patent of the phonograph, a cylinder covered with tin-foil on which sound waves could be recorded and from which they could be retrieved, together with Hertz's work on radio waves in 1888 and, in 1889, Berliner's first flat disc recording, prepared the way for all the development in audio in the twentieth century.

In 1900 Marconi demonstrated wireless telegraphy and the 1920s saw the various recording media perfected. In 1940 PVC tape became available and Philips cassettes in 1960.

Subsequent developments were talking newspapers and books for the blind and, more recently, laser beam recorded condensed discs.

Video

The important early discoveries that led to television and video included the observation, in 1873, of Joseph May, a telegraphist, who noticed that his equipment did not work properly in sunshine. This observation of the effect of light on selenium led on to the development of the photo-electric cell. The invention of the amplifying valve in 1896 and the cathode ray tube in 1897, were essential components, as was the 1923 patent of Vladimir Zworykin for an electronic camera, not then developed.

John Logie Baird, the Scottish inventor of television (1926) must be credited, also, with the concept of the disc-based video recording machine. In 1928 he devised a picture recording equipment in which a needle cut a groove into a revolving disc in response to electric pulses from a television camera, in a way similar to that of sound recording by electrical pulses coming from a microphone. Although the major part of present day video recording is on tape, the disc is the medium of the future.

In 1935 Baird Phonovision discs were put on sale. The BBC's first television service was in 1936. Colour television was developed in 1940 with a broadcast service starting in 1967. Black and white videotape recording was demonstrated in 1951, colour in 1957 and the disc recorder in 1968. Philips announced a *Laservision* video disc system in 1978 and this was commercially sold in the UK from 1982.

Telecommunications

A basic definition of the purpose of telecommunications is 'to transmit representations of information (signals) between remote locations'. Systems relevant to our subject gradually developed from 1862 when a still picture was first sent over a distance by wire, Amiens to Paris, and in 1908, London to Paris. The signal carriers can be electrical, electro-magnetic, or, since the 1970s, light waves. Optical fibre cables are the medium for transmitting light waves and the first public system in the UK started in 1980. The advantage of fibre optic links is that they are not subject to electrical or magnetic interference.

Since 1959, when a cable television system was tried out in Toronto, there have been many schemes to supply areas where normal transmissions are difficult to receive. They are not so necessary in the UK, but nevertheless are about to be further promoted and channels will include some for educational/library material.

Direct broadcasting by satellite could be a beneficial result of the successful 1958 US communications satellite launch. By 1986 the BBC will have channels using this technology via a European satellite. Programmes could be beamed to the satellite and back to a dish aerial on the roof of an agency for cable transmission to subscribers' sets.

Electronic-micrographic systems

By 1983, even the Eastman Kodak Company, which might have been thought to be for ever committed to totally film-based systems, was promoting micrographics equipment as 'the bridge to tomorrow's technologies'. Computer-assisted retrieval of microfilm and microfiche was being seen by Kodak as leading on to optical disc and microimage transmission by fibre optic carriers, but not before the next decade. Computer-assisted retrieval of microform documentation is the major, currently implemented, example of convergent technologies in information technology. Thus the data base, even in

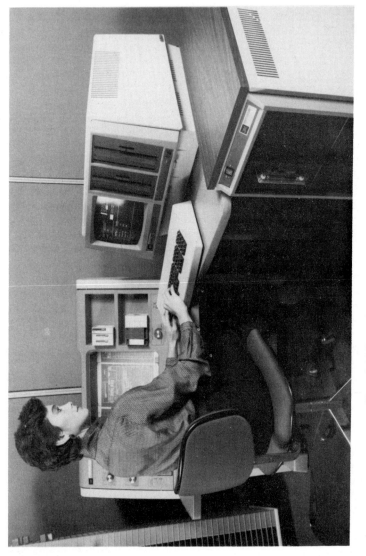

Figure 8.1 Micropoint computer and reader-printer (3M)

high volume document storage systems, continues to be stored on microfilm or microfiche with enormous advantages over other methods. These advantages reside in cost, storage capacity, reliability and archival quality (longevity).

In industry, commerce and government, office staffing costs have been contained by adopting computer assisted retrieval of micrographic copies of office documents. The time consuming work of filing and retrieval of paper documents is obviated. Documents are coded as they are produced, filmed, stored cheaply, retrieved and displayed as required. Computer-assisted retrieval encourages a systems approach to all office procedures before implementation. Given that the ultimate aim could well be the fully electronic office, then commencing with tackling the main office problem, ever-growing collections of paper documents, makes sense.

The library market for computer-assisted retrieval from micrographics systems is an additional, secondary market so far as equipment manufacturers are concerned; it is, nevertheless, a highly demanding market. Library needs are for full text storage and simple operation, with commands such as: *List, Display* and *Keep*. The micromputer element in some systems is limited to the indexing function, with screen display identifying the fiche or cassette number and the frame number required. The micrographic element then is manual selection and display in the microform viewer.

More expensive systems are fully automatic with selection by keyboard, microcomputer control and automatic display on the microform viewer. At present all these systems need both a cathode ray tube screen for the microcomputer and a microform viewing screen.

Image Systems markets a device comprising a carousel capable of holding 780 microfiches, giving it a capacity of up to 250 000 pages, retrievable by microcomputer in less than three seconds. In this system the microfiches are fitted with coded metal edge strips that enable accurate selection from random storage in the carousel. Imtec Ltd manufactures a retrieval system based on 16 mm microfilm with odometer read optical blips on the film and a keyboard by means of which to retrieve cassette and then frame. These two systems differ from each other in obvious ways, but they will serve as examples of what is available also from other manufacturers such as Kodak, Bell & Howell, 3 M, MAP, etc. One professional information provider, using computer assisted microfilm retrieval to enhance its services is *Derwent*.

The examples of computer-assisted retrieval so far noted are based on microfiche or microfilm but, of course, aperture cards and microfilm jackets are ideally suited to such systems. Jacket systems are cost effective for in-house operation where up-dating of documents is necessary. Either 16 mm or 35 mm microfilm, or both, can be housed in the standard A6 jacket. Amended information is refilmed, the film is cut up and the out-dated piece of film is pulled out from the fiche jacket and the newly filmed piece inserted in its correct place in the sequence of information, thus updating the file with new and/or corrected data. Descriptions of the seventy-six available systems using computer-assisted retrieval of microforms are published in an NRCd Report[3].

In view of the fact that space is now at a premium and reversion to the earlier naive assumption that libraries could and should grow indefinitely is unlikely, and even undesirable, the better equipped libraries, at least, should now be active in space economy measures. Computer-assisted retrieval of jacket microfiche copies of certain categories of publication is relatively cheap, can save space, improve the accuracy of indexing and retrieval and automate the filing of the information contained.

Pamphlets and reports are suitable library material with which to commence. Incoming pamphlets and reports could be microfilmed on 16 mm film using an existing planetary camera, and the originals discarded; thereafter the film can be cut and fitted into jackets. Alternatively a new machine of desk-top size can be acquired that will film in excess of 500 A4 documents per hour, at the same time processing the archival quality film and cutting it into strips ready for insertion into jackets.

The resultant jacket microfiche can be coded to exact frame and put into cassettes, each holding 30 microfiches and used on fast microprocessor-controlled retrieval units. Index information is displayed on the VDU screen and the full text of the selected document on the microfiche viewer screen.

Although such systems can be adopted gradually and in part, (e.g. by first adopting microcomputer selection with hand operation of the microform viewer), thus reducing the level of equipment funding required, librarians have been slow to progress in this direction.

Video provision in libraries now

The video formats to be found in libraries at the present time are Betamax, VHS, and Philips V2000. All are cassetted tape but they are incompatible, both in the way the tape is threaded in the cassette and in the path the tape takes in relation to the moving recording and replay heads.

A survey of public library provision made in mid-1982, with 160 libraries responding out of 167 circularised, revealed that 25 library

Figure 8.2 Interactive video disc instruction (Cameron)

systems were providing video lending services, 59 were actively considering doing so and 76 had decided against, at least for the time being[4]. Charges were made and the material was overwhelmingly for home entertainment with the motive of getting people, who would not otherwise do so, to visit their local library. Hiring out of the more ephemeral entertainment video cassettes could well be left to private enterprise unless a reasonable overall cost recovery charge is made. The matter of video material that is uncivilised in its depiction of violence, sex, etc., need not detain us here for, first, librarians would not knowingly select it for their libraries, and, secondly, existing laws against productions likely to deprave or corrupt have only to be more rigorously enforced in order to make its production unprofitable.

The growth field in library video lending provision will not be entertainment, but purpose made productions to instruct and stimulate the mind. There will, of course, also be a great deal of textual material. As yet there is little available, but entrepreneurs can be expected to develop the market. At the right time, existing micropublishers can be expected to convert their vast holdings of microform masters of printed texts to video disc format, but that is some way off at present.

Libraries serving educational institutions already have a much greater level of involvement in video than do public libraries, providing video cassettes, not normally for lending but for use on the library premises. As we have noted, these are both purchased and recorded off-air for current educational use. The latter are subsequently 'wiped' but proposed recording licensing arrangements may well affect the level of library provision.

There is at least one journal published *only* on video cassette, naturally in a subject in which visual material has a large role to play; this is the *Video Journal of Medicine*. One can expect a slowly growing number of such materials in libraries.

The Library Association has an Audio Visual Group that fosters the professional approach to these non-book materials and the American Library Association has a Video and Cable Communications Section.

It is normal to provide a special group television and video viewing room as part of library space provision and the requirements as to siting of these facilities are touched on in chapter 10.

Optical discs

The technology that we are concerned with here involves both high investment and high risk. Protection of investment demands the development of those innovations that are selected by a company and designed and invested in, and so standardisation will not even be considered until years later.

Thus, at the present time we have high priced optical disc systems available, with total incompatability between different makes right down to the discs themselves. The new technology is rife with many different practicable ways of achieving a given operational end, e.g. the recording process for optical discs, which in turn predicates differences in both reading heads and discs[5].

Even though some of these devices are now in operation, we can be sure that *general* implementation of optical disc information systems in libraries will not occur before the turn of the century. This does not mean that the promoters of this technology do not claim that it is all happening now — quite the contrary. We have quoted claims made by enthusiastic promoters of photographic microforms for the storage of massive quantities of information in complete desk-top libraries. Now manufacturers are actively promoting juke-box type desk sized equipment to house and play back up to five hundred optical digital discs. This would provide sufficient storage for the contents of a million books. The technology exists and the applications will follow. We have moved from the area of unsubstantiated assertion to possibilities and pilot projects. The social implications are immense. What the chosen applications will be remains to be seen, but large archives are the likely area whilst teaching and selling will further develop on interactive disc systems.

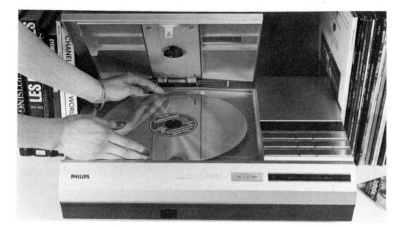

Figure 8.3 Laser disc player (Philips)

As there are several different types of optical disc devices on the market, of similar appearance but actually employing differing technological systems, it will suffice here to give a simple description of one example.

The disc is encoded with information by means of a laser beam burning microscopic 'pits' into the disc surface through to a metallised reflective film surface beneath. The 'pits', minute as they are, with several thousand to the inch, each represent the length of a laser pulse, which in turn is analogous to the original signal length, whilst the spaces between 'pits' represent the times when there is no laser pulse. The 'pits' are arranged on a spiral track.

In the reading head a tiny laser beam is focussed on to the reflective layer and thus dust on the top surface remains out of focus and does not interfere with the reading accuracy. The reflective surface reflects the beam back to a photo-sensor in the reading head which reacts differently to light and no-light caused respectively by a 'pit' through to the reflective layer or 'no pit'. These variations cause the generation of an electrical signal which represents the recorded data. It can readily be seen that binary coded digital data can be carried by impregnating, and retrieved by detection, of states of, 'pit' and 'no pit'.

Thus we have a very compact storage device indeed, on a 12 in or 305 mm disc. There is no mechanical wear on the disc as there is no stylus. The laser source used in reading is so minute compared with the recording beam, (0.4 mW as against 10 mW), that there is no degradation of the reflective surface by pitting in use. The lack of mechanical wear is vital, for the disc not only spins in selecting and retrieving the required information, but it also has to spin even to hold a still picture. It is a high precision technology with demanding tolerances on drive mechanisms. Flatness of disc is critical in focussing.

The storage capacity of optical digital disc is sixty to one hundred times more than an equivalent-sized magnetic disc. Manufacturers give greatly varying estimates as to the amount of data that can be carried. If an interactive mode is required the information capacity may well be halved to allow for it. One double sided optical disc can hold the equivalent of twenty-five magnetic tapes.

At the present time the major market for optical disc systems is for home entertainment. Philips *Laservision* is the prime example. It has to compete in the already established video tape market and has the disadvantage of being 'read only' with no recording capability. Its picture quality is technically much better than that of tape systems, but the material being marketed on disc at the time of writing is a sad collection of old films. The system can mix still pictures with motion picture sequences by self-switching, triggered by pulses on the disc; it has stereo sound. One available library application is *Video Patsearch* which combines on-line searching of patents with video disc display of drawings, chemical structures, etc.

Library applications of digital optical discs in the USA are in advance of those elsewhere. The Library of Congress has a pilot project in which digital optical discs will be used to provide high-density storage of the contents of books[6]. The urgent need for conservation of the contents of rapidly decaying books led to the decision to meet the high costs involved.

However, the project is very well worthwhile in its own right as a test of the new technologies available. One million pages will be scanned by an electronic digitiser over a two year period and stored on optical discs in juke-boxes. Access will be via the Library of Congress central computer, which will retrieve the desired pages for high resolution display and print-out. It is planned to overcome the problem of the short life span of optical discs by pressing new copies every few years. One expected benefit is that access time from optical disc on-line should be seconds as opposed to up to one hour now taken to find and present the actual book to the enquirer.

The Library of Congress has an existing optical disc system in which catalogue cards are printed at high speed to meet its DEMAND system for card purchasers world wide. The system laser scans cards, stores the images on optical discs and laser prints them at twelve cards per second.

Major advantages offered by these Library of Congress digital optical disc systems, to set against their very high cost, are seen to be space saving and conservation of the information content of libraries.

Interactive disc systems

Tape systems run through serially and can only be stopped, rewound, etc. A disc can be rapidly accessed at any point, making it ideal for interactive systems. By interactive video system is meant 'one in which the sequence and selection of messages is determined by the user's response to the material'[7].

Pioneers of interactive programmed instruction ranged from Sidney Pressey in the 1920s to Skinner and Crowder in the 1950s and the McGraw-Hill video disc experiment of 1977. Implemented interactive video disc schemes of the early 1980s include those of the *American Heart Association* and *Mothercare Ltd*. The American Heart Association system carries a full course on mouth-to-mouth resuscitation following cardiac arrest. The kit includes a dummy body fitted with sensors, which feed back information on how the student is doing. This information is both displayed on the screen and used by the microcomputer to interact with the video disc to display on the screen what should be done next. The interactive video disc system of Mothercare Ltd has two levels of programme, one with informative material to encourage customers to buy and the other to train staff in selling the same products.

The great advantage of tape systems over disc is their cheapness and easy local duplication possibilities. In addition to rapid access to any frame discs have unlimited still-frame capability, no disc wear, very fast scanning and precise finding, internal programming facility and very great storage density. However, one has to bear in mind the high cost, particularly of pressing the master. An excellent review of optical based document storage and retrieval systems appeared in *Reprographics Quarterly*, during 1983[8].

Videotext and Teletext

Videotext and Teletext developed as a means of using existing equipment, that is to say, telephones, computers, microcomputers and television receivers, for additional information purposes. The information carried is both text and graphics. The slow take-up of these facilities has led to the promotion of them in libraries and they have become a standard part of library provision. Up to the minute commercial information is an area of obvious need that these systems meet in business school libraries.

Teletext utilises television receivers to pick up and display data transmitted as part of ordinary broadcast television signals on the previously unused first five lines at the beginning of each television frame. An adaptor is necessary; it is not interactive. The BBC system *Ceefax* commenced in 1972 and the IBA system *Oracle* in 1973.

Videotext utilises telephone networks to carry signals from computerised storage to modems that convert them for viewing on a television screen or other terminal. It is made interactive by use of a keyboard. *Prestel*, the first public videotext system, opened in 1979 after trials in the previous year. At first, this British Telecom system had few subscribers — mainly business and library clients — and it still has not the predominance of home users for which it was planned. By the end of March 1984 there were 42 000 subscribers, 15 500 of them domestic. In 1982 a gateway service to link to external data suppliers' computers was instituted and in 1983 a telebanking system commenced. These services, particularly *Prestel*, have a growing role to play in libraries.

Much depends, however, on the information providers. At present there is not enough suitable material to constitute a really useful information source in higher education libraries. Availability at all hours is a minimal advantage which the telephone line based service, *Prestel*, has over services transmitted by television, i.e. *Ceefax* and *Oracle*, which are not on the air 24 hours a day. Academic institutions which are spread over more than one site can make use of a closed user group arrangement for their own information service on *Prestel*, and, of course, it could link university libraries if so desired.

Facsimile transmission

Telex has long had a role in academic libraries in providing rapid communication between researchers and in speeding loan requests. The obvious next step is facsimile transmission.

The older facsimile transmitters were analogue machines but the newer faster machines transmit digitised data and so are more economical of telephone time. An electronic scanner produces electronic signals that are decoded at the other end to produce a facsimile of the original document.

Book scanner and digitiser

The British Library has developed a book scanner and digitiser that can convert the text of books into digital form without harming valuable bindings. This has the dual purpose of conservation of the originals and the production of digital data that can be used in a data bank or for transmission.

Documents will tend to be digitised on production and put directly into data information systems, which will ease library access to material at present difficult to acquire.

Electronic publishing

All forms of non-traditional publishing, that is to say those forms which are not print on paper, have an in-built disadvantage to the author. The author's purpose usually includes a desire to be acknowledged financially, and, or academically, in that order.

'To reduce or eliminate publication and make information available from a store deprives scientists of the opportunity of obtaining evaluation by their colleagues, and thereby, of recognition and reward. Any proposal which diminishes or eliminates the easy achievement of recognition and reward is doomed to failure because of non-acceptance by authors'[9].

Thus the synoptic journal did not 'take-off'. The motives of the publishers are the obvious ones of wishing to remain in business and, if possible, to win a higher rate of return on their efforts. The user has yet a different purpose, that is, to acquire all the relevant information that can be discovered on the subject of the enquiry, as cheaply as possible, preferably without charge.

The conflict of interest between authors and publishers on one hand and the user of what is written and published on the other is potentially so great as to inhibit development, or, at the very least, to slow it down. New printing technologies have introduced far-reaching changes into the manner in which publishers operate. This technological upheaval, together with escalating labour costs and the perceived implications of information technology are major causes of the air of uncertainty about the future of *traditional* publishing. Indeed some publishers fear that printed paper journals will not be stocked by the library of the future and of course, if that proved to be the case, many journals could not be published in that format at all, libraries being the main purchasers. Hence the growing interest among publishers in the possibilities of electronic publishing.

If existing publishers were not actively considering how best to venture into electronic publishing and when, then computer, electronics and other interests could well usurp the publishing function. The Scientific Information Committee of The Royal Society in 1981 issued a report of a study of the UK scientific information system[10]. The major conclusion was that a combination of pressures was about to put the scholarly scientific publishing system under considerable strain. That the information system was in delicate balance rather than monumentally secure for all time needed stressing.

Some publishers believe, that in spite of the failure of synoptic microform publishing to make any impact on the market, new ways of packaging information, that is new formats will find additional markets. Also electronic publishing could change the way the author produces and uses information. The author could compose his article sitting at his microcomputer with word processing capability, edit it and send off the final version to a main frame computerised information service. He could retrieve the work of other writers and other 'published' data on-line without visiting the library. In this situation the hope of the publishers would be that payment would be made to them via automatic electronic transfer of funds. It may be thought, too, that reductions in library budgets would be less harmful to publishers, being offset by researchers 'logging-on' to electronically published journals as an integral part of the research process and funded accordingly.

It clearly is the case, as Vickery wrote as long ago as 1966, that there will be 'publications that originate in machine-readable form, are acquired and stored by the library in that form, and that never appear in visually legible form except on the screen of a user console'[11]. Taken to its logical final stage, the concept of the electronic transfer of information could produce a system that removed all need for traditional publishers, booksellers and librarians. The New Jersey Institute of Technology conducted an electronic journal pilot project between 1978 and 1980 with inconclusive results, although author attitudes were not favourable[12]. The British Library is funding a project, the Birmingham and Loughborough Network Development, which aims 'to identify the cost, capabilities and impact of an electronic journal and its associated information network'. At present it is seen by many to be more efficient to deliver print on paper, also, video reading is neither easy nor comfortable.

It is not satisfactory to have abstracts alone and full text needs to become the norm, available on-line after selection from abstracts. A progression from data base to data bank. To the existing problems of unauthorised and therefore non-revenue-producing copying, is added the ease of unauthorised, non-paying access to electronic systems. There is also the problem of electromagnetic pollution. We do not have the near certainty of purity of text that we have with print on paper and microphotography. Certainly, it is unlikely that types of publication already proving to be uneconomic in book format will ever revert to print once they have adopted a new medium.

A British government working group puts forward the view that electronic publishing 'will advance more quickly in directories, manuals and other publications which need frequent updating', but believes that growth will be 'gradual rather than dramatic'.

ADONIS

The Article Delivery Over Network Information System (ADONIS) was conceived as an on-demand facsimile journals article delivery system. This was set up in 1981 by a consortium of six publishers, namely, Academic Press, Blackwell Scientific, Elsevier, Pergamon, Springer and Wiley. By the end of 1983 no visible result had been achieved and only Blackwell Scientific, Elsevier and Springer remained in the consortium, with the others just maintaining interest. The next few years could see the commencement of a scheme much less ambitious than the original conception.

ADONIS was conceived as a data bank, storing full text scientific, technical and medical articles, with illustrations, including photographs in digital form on optical disc. It was hoped that some 3500 titles would be put into the system on publication. By charging for each document requested, a sum sufficient to enable part to be credited to the publisher of the journal in which the article appeared, royalty payments would in effect be levied on unwilling libraries. It was thought (by the publishers) that a change in the law of copyright might not then be necessary, and photocopying abuses would be limited.

It is possible that the withdrawal of some of the partners, mentioned above, was prompted by the hope that a new copyright act would enact fees from libraries for copying. Another possibility was that the Commission of European Communities project in electronic full text document delivery announced in November 1982 might absorb the costs of a full-scale trial project. Widespread interest in the subject is indicated by Pergamon's publication *Electronic Publishing Abstracts* being successfully launched. The *Project Intrex* of 1967, noted in chapter 3, predicted that, by 1975, facsimile transmission on-line based on computer access to microform would be the norm for journal articles. This was entirely correct as regards the available technology, but perhaps twenty-five years out as regards the likely general implementation.

References

1 CHARTRAND, R. L. and MORENTZ, J. W. (*eds*), *Information technology serving society*, Pergamon Press (1979)
2 BUXTON, H. W., *A memoir of the life of Charles Babbage*, 1871: a facsimile manuscript on 13 microfiches, Oxford Microform Publications Ltd

3 HENDLEY, A. M., *Automated/computer assisted retrieval of microforms: a guide and a directory*, 2nd ed, NRCd., (1983)
4 PINION, C. F., 'A survey of public library video involvement', *Library Association Record*, **85**, 1, January (1983)
5 WALTER, G., 'The optical digital data disc for . . . document storage, retrieval and electronic dissemination: a technological assessment', *Int. J. Micrographics & Video Technology*, 2, 4 (1984)
6 NUGENT, W. R. 'Applications of digital optical discs in library preservation and reference'. *Int. J. Micrographics & Video Technology*, 3, 1 (1984)
7 FLOYD, S. and B., (*eds*), *Handbook of interactive video*, Knowledge Industry Publications, (1982)
8 HENDLEY, A. M., 'Future optical based document storage and retrieval systems', *Reprographics Quarterly*, 16, 4 (1983) pp. 141–9
9 KILGOUR, F. G., 'Publication of scientific discovery: a paradox', in Black, D. V. (*ed*) *Proceedings of the 1966 ADI Annual Meeting*. Adrienne Press (1966) pp. 427–30
10 A study of the scientific information system in the UK: the report of a study undertaken by the Scientific Information Committee of the Royal Society . . . *BLR & D Report 5626*. The Royal Society 1981, 40 pp.
11 VICKERY, B. C., 'The future of libraries in the machine age'. *Library Association Record*, **68**, (1966) pp. 252–60
12 Electronic Document Delivery III. *Electronic publishing trends in the United States and Europe*, Learned Information for Commission of the European Communities. (1982) p. 31

Suggestions for Further Reading

1 BARRETT, R., *Optical video disc technology and applications: recent developments in the USA*. 43 pp. British Library (Library and Information Research Report 7) (1982)
2 BAHR, A. H., *Video in libraries: a status report, 1979–80*. 2nd ed. 119 pp. Knowledge Industry Publications Inc. (1980)
3 CHING-CHIH CHEN and BRESSLER, S. E., *Microcomputers in libraries*. 266 pp. Neal-Schuman Publishers Inc/Mansell Publishing Ltd. (1982)
4 SIGEL, E., *et al*. *Video discs: the technology, the applications and the future*. 183 pp. Knowledge Industry Publications Inc (1980)

Nine

Archival potential of non-book media

Microforms

The *Genealogists' Magazine* of September 1981 noted a comment by the Archivist of the United States:

> 'Before placing full reliance on microfilm, or any other non-paper medium, we need to be certain that it will save money, and, more importantly, that it will outlast the paper. In spite of our space problems, which may never really be solved, archivists will ponder a long time before they recommend destruction of original records'.

His concern stemmed from the fact that non-book media, with the exception of silver halide microfilm, bring no assurance of the longevity that top quality paper carries. Handmade paper has, in some instances, lasted for centuries. Machine made paper, on the other hand, is normally made from wood pulp, and, since the 1860s has included alum with the wood fibres. The alum produces sulphuric acid by reacting with moisture in the atmosphere, thus degrading the paper. For the future, the answer is to use acid-free paper for all documents and books of interest exceeding twenty-five years.

Microfilming is, at present, the only safe way of ensuring the survival of decaying archival records and the vast stocks of 19th century books that are so rapidly decaying in our national and university libraries. A. M. Hendley, of the National Reprographic Centre for documentation, in a report that should be studied by all archivists and librarians, states: 'Of the four media reviewed in this report (paper, microfilm, magnetic tape and optical data discs), only high grade paper and silver halide microfilm can be regarded as archival[1]'.

Non-silver films, diazo and vesicular, are cheaper to produce. Diazo is a polyester-based film containing a diazonium salt layer. It is exposed to u.v. light through a silver master and the copy is developed using ammonia, either in solution or dry. Diazo copies of positives remain positives. Vesicular microfilm is also polyester based with a diazonium salt layer, but when it is exposed to u.v. light tiny bubbles of nitrogen are formed. These bubbles, after heat treatment, scatter light in the exposed areas, whilst unexposed areas remain clear. The image is a reversed copy of the original. The major advantage of vesicular film is that its development process does not require chemicals and thus it can be processed in air conditioned rooms where ammonia would not be acceptable.

Although silver halide is the proven archival quality film, diazo, even in the absence of adequate testing of it and other types by the passage of time in normal use, has become widely used for microfiche duplicates. Library catalogues and regularly updated office documentation can well be produced on diazo microfiche, for timeliness is the keynote and there is always a duplicate set of fiches and a magnetic tape or disc stored elsewhere. Most other library material, however, is regarded as an investment in stock-building and needs to be of archival quality.

Government departments such as the Public Record Office sell microform copies of their documents on diazo rather than silver halide on the grounds that microfiche copies of archival records are, more often than not, ordered by libraries for the immediate use of one or two scholars and therefore librarians should be more concerned with acquiring the microfiche cheaply and quickly rather than with an assured standard of archival permanence. Thus, even if the diazo should fade, the fact that the Public Record Office or other issuing authority holds masters from which replacements can readily be produced, should, it is suggested, defuse any protest from librarians.

It may well be that government agencies have come to a valid assessment of the ephemeral nature of much of the vast output of present day government documents, but the older material certainly needs to be available on silver halide. In 1982, 53 000 documents, or 75% of the US Government Printing Office output, was available on diazo microfiche, some being available only in that form. In defence of diazo, it is recorded that a six month exposure to bright sunlight on a window ledge in Singapore University Library merely yellowed a diazo microfiche, but did not reduce its legibility. However conclusive that test might appear, librarians would be most unwise, in the absence of adequate scientifically based tests, to buy books, periodicals or data services on a microfilm base that is not of proven archival permanence, unless usage needs are known to be short term.

Certain micropublishers, are anxious to get libraries not to discriminate against diazo, presumably because their profits on this type of film are more advantageous to them. Some vesicular film has, in the past, given libraries problems in the emission of gas during storage. The gas has become mixed with air and moisture, producing hydrochloric acid which has eaten into the film storage containers. The trouble, it is said, was limited to one type of film sold between 1967 and 1970 and the defect should not recur. Clearly, however, librarians must specify their needs and the norm should be film of proven archival quality under normal conditions of use and storage, that is, conditions not subject to extremes of temperature and humidity.

Allen B. Veaner of *Microform Review* has consistently reminded librarians of the need to insist on silver halide stock. He 'urges readers to question the introduction of non-silver micrographic materials and processes prior to the adoption of standards governing their processing and testing[2]'. The National Reprographic Centre for documentation has reported on a project for 'Determining the storage life of diazo and vesicular film'. It is probable that UK libraries should specify that they will normally buy only silver halide microforms as a result of these findings. Briefly, it was found that diazo, exposed to light in a reading machine, together with some ambient light in use, does fade relatively quickly[3].

The Resources and Technical Services Division of the American Library Association, in July 1975 recommended that US libraries 'buy for their permanent collections only microforms (such as silver halide film) for which standards for archival permanence have been established by recognised standards organisations'. There was also an American National Standards Institution experiment where the life of diazo films in dark storage was compared with that of silver halide films. This experiment demonstrated, by extrapolation, useful life expectancies of 9–140 years for the diazo films — but no discernible deterioration in the silver halide film[4].

As regards microforms in colour, I believe they have no archival permanence. Just as our coloured travel slides fade at periods varying between five and thirty years, depending on factors including the amount of use — i.e. exposure to light and heat in a projector — and the care taken by the photographic firm in processing, so also coloured microforms will not be guaranteed.

Inevitably, a long-established use of microfilm has been that in public archives. The object of this filming, as is the case with rare books, is to remove the need to handle the original. Thus due regard to the conservation of originals requires expert filming at the first attempt. A good master film is essential in order to enable the wider use of unique historical material by replicating the film. The Public Record Office, County Record Offices and Public Reference Libraries all make extensive use of microfilm as a means of providing public access to parish, town, county and national records. Every central public library should have microfilms of the census returns of the district, 1841 to the last date released, all the parish registers, town plans, poll lists and local directories of earlier years, as well as maps of historical interest and local charters.

Many of the earlier films of parish records in the UK were poorly filmed and the author writes this as a considerable user of them. The poor quality of the film is an indication, in some cases, of the difficulty of the task and of the need for it to be expertly done. Often we are dealing with hand-written documents, with ink of all shades of black, brown and, by now, yellow, on paper of shades of white, yellow and grey. The thickness of the paper varies so that, on occasion, it allows confused glimpses of what is written on the back of the sheet. Often there is present crumpling, some tearing, damp and fire damage marks. Some bindings are very tight, giving difficulty with overall focus.

As I have stressed, the purpose of filming was to conserve the originals whilst providing the best possible copies. It therefore follows that many of these early poor quality films should now be replaced after expert refilming of the original documents. Valuable archive material should be filmed 'in house', even if by contract, because only thus can one keep the necessary control over handling. Filming technique is now vastly better with control of exposure of each frame determined by the needs of each area of the surface by multiple electric cells within the modern planetary camera.

If it is important to ensure good filming of archive material, equally the viewing equipment should be first class and modern. Often it is not, and there is an air of clanking, whirring and creaking in archive reading rooms — but this is changing. Ease of operation, good optical quality and ease of control of focus and luminance and 360° image rotation are of immense importance in influencing the general acceptance of microform retrieval methods where they are appropriate, as in the case of archives.

If the apparatus is not up to first class standard, a programme of re-equipping should be set in hand. The standard of cleanliness of the lenses, glasses and screens should be watched and a scheme of regular cleaning enforced. As in other areas of microform reading, the staff in the archive office, search room and reference library should be instructed not to apologise to users that records are available only on microfilm. Rather they must ensure that all first-time users are instructed on how to get a reading machine into operation efficiently and swiftly.

Magnetic tape archives

The application of information technology has produced a growing flood of magnetic tape archives. The inherent nature of computer tapes as miniaturisations of data has encouraged underestimation of the areas of storage required and, together with lack of experience, has led to the use of unsuitable locations for storage.

In noting that these faults related to US Federal Government Departments in general, a 1971 report went on to state that the likely longevity of data on magnetic tape was 18–24 months and annual recopying was recommended. A former Assistant Archivist of the United States wrote:

'There is no agreement among tape librarians and manufacturers as to how long magnetic tape will hold its magnetic signals, even assuming the best care is given to the tape from the date of purchase . . . The National Bureau of Standards . . . has found that tape stored from one to seven years can be expected to show varying rates of error. Magnetic tape in storage can be subject to a long list of ills. The storage itself tends to set the tape more firmly in any physical imperfection such as occurs from cinching, cupping, skewing, overhanging, buckling, ridging, etc. Exposure to any magnetic field is disastrous to tape, and even proximity to electrical fixtures and conduits can do harm. Tape cannot be stored in any building near nuclear or electrical generating or radiation facilities, and it is also susceptible to damage by lightning. High temperature or high humidity can damage tape beyond salvage, as can rough handling, dropping or improper packing for shipment . . . Magnetic tape is too fragile, ephemeral or impermanent to be a medium for the preservation of data of permanent value'.[5]

Another authority writes:

'Ideally archival storage should retain information essentially for ever without requiring any power, be inexpensive, have good handling properties, and be physically immune to any failures that might destroy its contents. It usually does not have to be accessed rapidly, but it must be reliable. At present we do not know of any materials that possess all these qualities to an adequate degree . . . The shelf-life of the information stored on magnetic tape (including videotape) is not very good (and often not predictable *a priori*) because of bleed-through and other problems. Archival storage is typically written once and read an arbitrary number of times. The ability to rewrite magnetic tape is not a great advantage in the context of archival storage, in fact, because of the danger of erasure, tape presents a disadvantage in this case. Microfilm, holograms, and any other inexpensive write-once, read many times media are preferable from this point of view[6]'.

Magnetic disc archives

Magnetic disc likewise has poor archival potential, for its electro-magnetic state can be changed by design or accident, thus losing the data stored. Analogue data once lost, or largely damaged, is irretrievable.

To seek to ensure even the restricted life that might reasonably be expected of magnetic disc, the storage environment must be controlled. Copying discs at intervals is the only long-term safeguard.

Optical disc and tape

Suppliers would not claim more than ten years life expectancy nor guarantee more than two to three years for optical tape and disc. Again, as for the magnetic media, the storage environment is of great importance and copying is advised to meet long-term needs.

Conditions necessary for archival storage .

Microforms have been present in libraries long enough for us to know that provision for their preservation is not too demanding. If we meet the advocated conditions for the safe storage of micro-forms, then, with one or two additions, they represent the minimum provision necessary for the storage of the other non-book media.

The ideal storage is an air-conditioned room, in order to avoid excessive heat and high humidity, a combination of which can lead to destruction of film and tape by fungi or bacteria. A temperature of between 16–27°C (60–80°F) is advised. The massive archive of microfilm masters held by University Microfilms Inc. is kept in air-conditioned vaults at 70°F with 40% humidity. Should air conditioning not be available, then, in temperate climates such as that of the UK, storage in separate containers in tightly closed drawers, cabinets or cupboards, in which there is placed a desiccator of silica gel is recommended.

In addition to temperature and humidity, chemical factors are covered by British Standard 1153[7], but the environmental enemies of books are those of all library media — dust, humidity, high temperature, damp and sulphurous atmosphere. Thus, providing we add the requirement to avoid magnetic sources, electric conduits, etc as well as a ban on smoking, a standard work on archival storage, such as Joyce Banks' *Guidelines for preventive conservation*, will give a detailed guide to storage needs[8]. The suggestions given by Banks are: pollution free air; a temperature of 19–20°C; 50% relative humidity; acid-free containers; regular cleaning programme; no eating or drinking in the store; storage lighting, 10–30 lux; reading room lighting, 100 lux; avoidance of u.v. sources (natural and fluorescent lighting); and use non-reactive separate containers. These containers should not be piled one upon the other but stored on end on shelves or in cabinets.

Standards

Standards, national and international, clearly cannot be compulsory, but are accepted voluntarily where they are observed at all. Nevertheless, the very existence of standards, duly considered, agreed by interested parties and published, leads to the gradual elimination of pointless variations and avoids perpetuating, indefinitely, known shortcomings and faults.

'Interested parties' includes strong representation of the industry, as of course, they need to be in broad agreement with what is proposed. The representatives of the industry are usually technical experts, who engage in a dialogue with selected users and between them appropriate standards are evolved. Thus one hopes that the possibility of good technical performance for the product is built into the specifications.

The appropriate standards should always be checked and specified by the librarian when selecting equipment for purchase and in contracts for production of all non-book media. The emphasis placed by librarians on the need for consistently effective quality control by micropublishers of their products has undoubtedly proved fruitful. It is probable that in the past micropublishers considered that librarians were seeking to lay down excessively exacting standards. It may have appeared adequate to the publisher to adopt minimal control procedures and to undertake to replace imperfect film when actual use revealed a blemish. This would have negated the archival purpose of purchasing the microfilm in the first place, for initial use some years after purchase of early back issues of certain learned journals might uncover illegible text at the time of need to use it. The influence of the Microform Association of Great Britain, the Library Association and similar bodies in other countries in having members active on standards panels has been effective.

Microform and video standards quite naturally, are of much wider application than to library materials alone, and, of course, there will not be standards produced for the information devices of the newer technologies until they are generally applied and present in libraries. That time will be when the initial investment in research and development has been recouped and profits have started to come in. The following is a list of relevant British Standards Institution micrographics standards, with International Standards numbers in brackets, where appropriate.

BS 1153:1975	Recommendations for the processing and storage of silver-gelatin type microfilm (ISO 2803)
BS 1371:1973	Specification for 35 and 16 mm microfilms, spools and reels (ISO 1116)
BS 4187	Specification for microfiche
Part I:1981	60 frame format (ISO 2707)
Part II:1973	98 frame format (ISO 2707)
Part III:1978	Formats of 208, 270, 325, 420 frames (except COM)
BS 4189:1967	Specification for conventional typographic characters for legibility (ISO 435)
BS 4191:1976	Specification for microform readers
BS 4210:1977	Specification for 35 mm microcopying of technical drawings (ISO 3272)
Part I	Operating procedures
Part II	Photographic requirements for silver film
Part III	Unitised microfilm carriers
BS 4657:1970	Methods of determining the resolution obtained in microcopying (ISO 3334)
BS 5444:1977	Recommendations for preparation of copy for microcopying
BS 5513:1977	Specification for 35 mm microcopying of newspaper cuttings on A6 microfiche
BS 5525:1977	Specification for 35 mm microcopying of maps and plans
BS 5536:1978	Preparation of technical drawings and diagrams for microfilming
BS 5632:1978	Specification for microfilm jackets A6 size
BS 5644:1978	Specification for computer output microfiche (COM) A6-size (ISO 5126)
BS 5687:1979	Recommendations for storage conditions for silver image photographic plates for record purposes
BS 5699:1979	Processed photographic film for archival purposes
Part I	Silver-gelatin type on cellulose ester base
Part II	Silver-gelatin type on poly (ethylene terephthalate) base
BS 5847:1980	Specification for 35 mm microcopying of newspapers for archival purposes (ISO 4087)

BS 5956:1980	Specification for A6-size microfiche for the motor industry
BS 5976:1980	Specification for the density of silver-gelatin type microfilms (ISO 6200)
BS 6054	Glossary of terms for micrographics (ISO 6196)
Part I:1981	General terms
Part II:1983	Image positions and methods of recording
Part III:1984	Film processing
BS 6313:1982	35 mm microcopying of serials
BS 6342:1983	Specification for 105 mm microcopying of technical drawings (single image A6-size)
BS 6354:1983	Specification relating to the method for measuring the screen luminance, contrast and reflectance of microform readers
BS 6359:1983	Specification for dimensions and position of microfiche heading coating (colour stripe)

Video applications in libraries are relatively recent and although there are technical standards such as BS 4967:1983, BS 5818:1979, BS 5819:1980 and BS 6411:1983, it is likely that the only video standards of possible general interest here are:

BS 5817:1980	Audio-visual, video and television equipment and systems: Part I, General. Part II, Explanation of general terms.
BS 6311:1982	Measuring television or tape machine parameters
BS 6412:1983	Measurement of video tape properties

Quality control

Quality control in micropublishing does not begin at the point of checking the finished product, it commences at the setting up stage. The text to be photographed has to be collated for completeness and legibility. The focus of the camera, the film itself, the chemicals used in processing, their mix, specific gravity, temperature, etc., all need regular checking.

Procedures have to be set up to monitor all these matters as regular routine production line procedures. Master negatives need to be checked page by page for completeness of text. Densities need checking and scratches and spots found and refilming arranged as necessary. Thereafter printing-masters and copies ordered by customers are produced from these master negatives and they are subjected to the same quality checking system.

It is of little use preparing microforms to archival standards if the materials in which they are packed for despatch and storage can cause film decay. Thus, standards as to pH neutrality, etc., have to be enforced in the matter of quality control of packaging.

Preparation of video publications needs the same level of control for accuracy and quality if they are to be effective information media, even though they will not be of 'archival quality'.

References

1   HENDLEY, A. M., *The archival storage potential of microfilm, magnetic media and optical data discs*, Hatfield, NRCd. (1983)
2   VEANER, A. B., 'An ominous trend?', *Microform Review*, 4, 9 (1975)
3   BROADHURST, R. N., *An investigation of the effects of exposure to light on diazo microfilm*, NRCd. (1976)
4   *Reprographics Quarterly*, 11, 3 (1978)
5   ALLDREDGE, E., *Records Management Journal*, (1970) No. 6
6   DOLOTTA, T. A., *et al, Data processing in 1980–1985*, Wiley, (1976)
7   BS 1153:1975, *Recommendations for the processing and storage of silver-gelatin type microfilm*, London. BSI (1975)
8   BANKS, J. M., *Guidelines for preventive conservation*, prepared by Joyce M. Banks. Ottawa, Committee on Conservation/Preservation of Library Materials (1981)

Ten

Aids for the user and the librarian

Cataloguing

The librarian must expect the cataloguing of microforms and other non-book media to be more time-consuming than is the cataloguing of books. In the longer term one will find much more of this material being catalogued centrally and the details added to the mechanised cataloguing data bases.

The Library of Congress cataloguing in publication scheme includes micropublications and they are accorded full bibliographical treatment and MARC input as for books. In the case of the audio-visual materials, however, the Library of Congress does not catalogue all of them. It is likely that it will be considered convenient to have a separate catalogue of microforms in the main microform reading areas of a library. Likewise separate catalogues will probably be compiled for each category of audio-visual material, but the fact that there are separate catalogues does not make it any the less desirable to enter such stock in the main catalogues also.

There is the same need for the catalogue entries relating to non-book materials to be as useful finding aids as the entries relating to books. Thus, the equivalent in finding value of standard author and subject cataloguing is necessary for each format. There are but two significant differences and they are related:

1 Because the format is different and there is a need to use the media on the appropriate equipment, the catalogue entry must state either 'on microfilm' or 'on microfiche', 'on micro-opaques', or 'video cassette', 'video disc' etc.
2 Because the format involves different access arrangements, the finding mark will refer to this rather than to a subject classification. Thus there will be shelving categories:

microfilm periodicals; microfilm dissertations;
microfiche periodicals; microfiche dissertations;
microfiche reports; microfiche monographs;
micro-opaque series; video cassettes; video discs, etc.

These will be indicated on the catalogue cards, as appropriate, by suitable symbols.

There is an alphabetical coding system of the physical formats of audio-visual materials, devised by Malcolm Shifrin, that, in due course, will work its way into general use via the BLAISE data AVMARC, as more of this material becomes recorded in the automated cataloguing system.

Just as, in the case of books, the catalogue entry will detail the number of volumes and pages, the entry for a non-book medium publication needs to indicate whether negative or positive, how many reels of film or, how many microfiche. If the item is printed paper format plus microfiche, it needs to state the number of pages plus the number of microfiches. For video the number of cassettes, whether black and white or in colour etc are requisite. As with all other library material, an entry should appear at the appropriate place in the classified or other subject catalogue.

Certain microform series, such as the ERIC and NASA microfiches, do not need individual cataloguing of each item because normal access is by serial number as given in published listings. Periodicals need to be entered both in the periodicals catalogue and in the separate microform catalogue. If the cataloguing of non-book media is to be effective, it has to be accompanied by efficient guiding and labelling of storage containers.

Titles in microform sets

Publishers' collections must be adequately catalogued. The problem about these is, of course, that potentially they can equate to the acquisition of a whole additional library at a stroke. Thus co-operative cataloguing arrangements are likely to be necessary. On the publisher's part adequate listing and printed paper indexes are essential.

The University of California Library at Riverside has a cataloguing project and sells to other libraries sets of its catalogue cards. They offer various options such as one card for each title included in one of these elephantine collections or complete sets of three cards for each work in the microform library. Examples of sets for which the University of California Library offers this service are *American Culture* and *Three Centuries of Drama*.

The US Association of Research Libraries commissioned a study, 1981–83, to discover how best to establish bibliographical control over titles in microform sets. Their publication, *Cataloguing Titles in Microform Sets* describes *inter alia* the *ARL Microform Project*. Greatly underused, it was clear that microform collections published in sets need full analytical cataloguing in order to make known what is available. Development in the USA of on-line cataloguing via networks, provided the encouragement to plan for the cataloguing of each microform set once only, on a co-operative basis, for the benefit of all. This was clearly necessary as libraries that had carried out the individual cataloguing of each title in the sets they purchased, had reported resulting large increases in use of material in sets. The co-operative cataloguing data produced is fed into data bases such as OCLC.

Chapter seven of the second edition of the *Anglo-American Cataloguing Rules*[1] applies to the cataloguing of video and other similar materials. There is also *Standards for Cataloguing Non-print Materials*, published by the Association for Educational Communication and Technology.

Sources of information on publications

Microforms

In addition to the lists issued by micropublishers discussed in chapter 4, libraries need to acquire some at least of the publications listed below. These are the general bibliographical guides to micropublishing.

Guide to Microforms in Print. An annual publication of Microform Review Inc., that is now established as the bibliography of available micropublications throughout the world. There are English, French, German and Spanish versions of the Introduction, an alphabetical list of publishers and a directory of publishers arranged by the letter codes used in the volume, together with their addresses. The main body of the guide is an alphabetical arrangement of authors and titles. There are numbered categories by means of which one can determine whether the title is on film, fiche or card, its size, coloured or black and white. Prices are of course given. It is published in the UK by Mansell Information/Publishing Ltd.

Subject Guide to Microforms in Print is the essential complementary volume to the *Guide* noted above. The subject arrangement is by broad subject groups. The details given are exactly as in the *Guide*. The address of Microform Review Inc. is 520 Riverside Avenue, P.O. Box 405, Saugatuck Station, Westport, Ct. 06880, USA, and Mansell Information/Publishing Ltd is at 6 All Saints St., London. N1 9RL. The former is the publisher and the latter is the agent outside North and South America for both these guides.

The Library of Congress publishes two useful items. These are *Newspapers on Microfilm*, which lists newspapers by geographical location, subarranged by strict title order, and *National Register of Microform Masters*. The register is an annual that has, since 1970, been a one-sequence arrangement of monographs and serials (other than newspapers) in alphabetical order. It is not complete, in that libraries sometimes neglect to send in details of the microform masters that they hold. It is important to note that it is not cumulative and lists masters only, so it is useful only as an indicator of the whereabouts of master microforms in the Library of Congress and other US and Canadian libraries. The entries carry Library of Congress numbers. *The National Register of Microform Masters* is available from Library of Congress, Washington DC 20540, USA.

Two micropublishers issuing monumental annual lists of microforms published by others as well as themselves deserve mention here. University Microfilms International publishes a 900 page, 13 000 title, *Serials in Microform*, available on microfiche as well as in printed paper format. *Books on Demand*, is UMI's catalogue of masters held from which copies can be produced for customers, on demand. Microforms International Marketing Corporation lists, annually, the output of 169 micropublishers. Available to libraries, gratis, MIMC's *Microforms Annual* has more than 670 pages in its 6th edition, 1984/85. It is in three parts. Part I, *Scholarly Serial Publications* has 499 pages in double columns and 17 319 entries. The more recent periods for which microforms are available are listed separately from the older volumes in order to ease the task of selection. Part II, *Special Microform Projects*, is of 130 pages and lists the large microform projects undertaken over the years by MIMC. It now lists, also, Oxford Microform Publications' projects. Full descriptions are given of imaginative micropublishing ventures such as the *Malthus Collection*. Part III *Current Serials and Related Microforms* completes the catalogue.

Microform Market Place is an international directory of micropublishing, published by Microform Review Inc. in North and South America and elsewhere by Mansell Information Publishing Ltd., address as given above.

The Micropublishers' Trade List Annual is another Microform Review Inc. publication and is made up of microfiche reproductions of micropublishers' catalogues. It aims to be a complete file of US and other companies.

Microform Review has, since its first volume in 1972, proved to be just the sort of journal that librarians with responsibility for microform provision should read regularly. It is a quarterly, in printed paper and microfiche format and has an annual index. It carries well-written authoritative articles on all aspects of microform use. *Microform Review* is particularly valuable in selecting series appearing in microform, for it evaluates each in relation to the same sixteen points. Thus, in addition to the microformat, the librarian will always know the film type, reduction ratio, indexing provided, etc. The regular make-up of the *Review* comprises: comments and news, informative articles, microform reviews, book reviews, materials in simultaneous publication, recent articles on micropublishing, clearinghouse of library microform projects and index.

The comments and news, as one would expect, are largely American, but as the USA is the largest single microform market with a great deal of current growth, this section is of great interest to UK and European readers. The clearing house section lists library microfilming projects. These are in the main collections of papers deposited in learned libraries that are being micropublished to improve availability. Details of availability of microform copies and price are given. The Editor-in-Chief is Allen B. Veaner, Librarian of the University of California at Santa Barbara, and the Technical Editor is Hubbard W. Ballou of Columbia. It is published by Microform Review Inc., 520 Riverside Avenue, P.O. Box 405, Saugatuck Station, Westport, Connecticut 06880, USA.

International Journal of Micrographics and Video Technology, Pergamon Press, 1982 to date, carries articles and news on micropublishing and reviews books and microform publications.

The Microfiche Foundation is an international non-profitmaking organisation housed in the Delft Technological University Library, the Netherlands. It has as its aim the propagation of the use of microfiche, not only in the library and university world but also in industry, commerce and for the private individual who wants to build up his own collection in this form. The *Microfiche Foundation Newsletter* is published approximately three times a year. The articles are authoritative and illustrated. There is an informative and illustrated new equipment section, a Microfiche Bibliography and Publications on Microfiche. The address is 101 Doelenstraat, Delft, the Netherlands.

Video formats

Videodisc/Videotex, Volume 1, 1981 to date published by Meckler Publishing, address as above, carries reviews of video projects of all sorts set out in the manner used by *Microform Review*. Thus comparison of projects and ready discovery of information is facilitated.

The Video Source Book has been published annually since 1979 by The National Video Clearinghouse. There is also *Video Source Book – U.K.* (since 1981) from the same publisher and from Bookwise Video in the U.K. A useful list of *U.K. Video Producers and Distributors* appeared in the *International Journal of Micrographics & Video Technology*, Volume 3, number 1, 1984[2]. Other indexes to available video material are: *Chicorel Index to Video Tapes and Cassettes, Index to Educational Videotapes* and *Update of Non-book Media*, the latter two from the National Information Centre for Education Media (USA), and *North American Film and Video Directory* (Bowker).

Other guides with a wider audio-visual coverage are: *British National Film Catalogue* (British Film Institute), *HELPIS*, (British Universities Film Council), *Audio-Visual Materials for Higher Education*, (BUFC) and the *British Catalogue of Audio-Visual Materials* (British Library, BSD).

Sources of information on equipment

The best source of information on equipment, both micrographic and related information technologies, is the National Reprographic Centre for documentation, attached to the Hatfield Polytechnic, but separately housed at Bayfordbury, Hertford, SG13 8LD. Government financed, NRCd is independent and its technical evaluations of equipment can be relied upon to be unbiased. Evaluations of individual items and groups of equipment are published cheaply. NRCd also runs practical technical courses.

Reprographics Quarterly is the journal of the National Reprographic Centre for documentation. It bears on its title page '. . . the applications and technology of micrographic, reprographic and other new media for documentation'. It has a news and editorial section which is balanced, well informed and refreshingly independent in outlook. There are authoritative articles and major sections, 'Evaluation' and 'First Look', each dealing with new equipment. There is an abstracts section.

The *International Journal of Micrographics & Video Technology*, Vol. 1, 1982 to date (Pergamon Press) carries articles on the inter-related advances in electronic information transfer in micropublish-ing, electronic journals, photographic and video including exploita-tion of data bases by these means.

Videoinfo and *Microinfo* are twin, very well informed newsletter-type publications from Microinfo Ltd., PO Box 3, Newman Lane, Alton, Hants. GU34 2PG.

The *British Micrographic Manufacturers Association Product Guide* provides a conspectus of British made micrographics equipment, with names and addresses of manufacturers.

Videodisc/Videotex, Volume 1, 1981 to date, (Meckler) provides informative illustrated articles of current practice in this field.

The *International Information Management Congress* was founded in 1963 as the *International Micrographics Congress* with Eugene B. Power as one of its founders. With the manufacturing side of micrographics largely American based, the aim was to assist manu-facturers in promoting the industry. Undoubtedly, in moving round the world and staging its conferences and exhibitions of equipment in key communications centres it made the capabilities of micro-graphics systems better known. More recently its change of title has indicated the widening of the manufacturers' interests into informa-tion technology in general. Its publications, *IMC Journal* and *IMC Newsletter* carry details of equipment and systems.

The *Journal of Information and Image Management* reflects the NMA's change of name from National Micrographics Association to *Association for Information and Image Management*. Thus it is the Journal of Micrographics extended to reflect the manufacturers interests in all the convergent information technologies.

Micrographics Equipment Review is a Microform Review publica-tion, a quarterly that commenced in 1976. Its aim is to assist in equipment purchasing decisions, by reviewing suitable equipment. There is also a useful *International Micrographics Source Book* available in the UK from NTIS, PO Box 3, Newman Lane, Alton, Hants. GU34 2PG. It is published by Microfilm Publishing Inc.

Microcopie 84: Le Guide de L'Acheteur is the standard guide to the French micrographics industry. Available from 11, rue de

Provence, 75009, Paris, it lists addresses of micropublishers, distributors, service bureaux. Over 1000 products are arranged by category. The major French micrographics journal, *Le Courier de la Microcopie*, is available from the same publisher.

Three other established guides to equipment are: *Audio Visual Equipment Directory* (National Audio Visual Association, USA), *Audio Visual Market Place* (Bowker) and *The Video Register* (Knowledge Industry Publications).

There are two titles first published in 1984, that promise to be very useful as guides to the selection of equipment in the whole range of the information technologies covered by this book. First, there is *The Electronic Media Directory and New Media Yearbook*, (1984), published by WOAC Communications Company of Dunstable.

The second, and much more important, publication of 1984 is *Barbour – Builder Product Selector: The Automated Office*. It is an annual supported by a periodical newsheet and a telephone enquiry service at £85 per annum. Its 466 pages are divided into sections each dealing with a different category of equipment relevant to the electronic library. There are sections on micro- and minicomputers, equipment for data input and its output, telecommunications micrographics, printing, etc. There has long been a need for an annual handbook that tabulates comparable equipment in categories with the manufacturers'/answers to the same questions about each product, including indication of compatibilities and one-off price. This publication meets that need for the UK market. Each section begins with an options page where the type of equipment available and its characteristics are outlined, followed by a detailed tabulation of what is available. Barbour–Builder Ltd publish from New Lodge, Drift Road, Windsor, Berks SL4 4RQ.

Ergonomics

An ergonomic evaluation of visual display terminals reported in *Behaviour & Information Technology*[3] found that examination of eight terminals showed essential differences for all the parameters, which might be partially responsible for eye strain and postural complaints. The writers recommend that customers should pay more attention to ergonomic qualities when choosing a terminal, and at the same time 'look for proper design of the whole work station including the working environment'[3]. The greatest problem with screens of VDTs is the tendency for them to be unduly small. Other matters to watch are oscillation, sharpness and stability of

characters. Luminance and its contrast with other screens, documents and ambient lighting levels, reflectance from the screen and
the keyboard are important items to check as are the size and positioning possibilities of the keyboard.

Operators should have eye tests *before* being employed on visual
display units and at regular intervals thereafter. Visual discomfort
of operators must be avoided and persons with eye defects should
not be employed on this work, otherwise complaints of eye blurring,
eye soreness and double images can be made. Radiation energy
several magnitudes higher than that emanating from a VDU would
be required before there could be risk of damage to cornea or lenses
of the eye. Posture is important, appropriate seat height, wrist rests
and adjustable screen angles are essential matters for consideration.

The microform viewing equipment experience of the last few
years has revealed certain irreversible trends. On the better equipment text is displayed at full size without glare caused by uneven
screen luminance or visible light sources. There is precise focusing
with good contrast and resolution. Screens are angled and have
some hooding. There are easy to reach controls and variable illumination level and two-speed facility on motorised viewers.

Plastic cases are well designed and the compact lighting units are
easily removed for lamp replacement. Tungsten halogen lamps of
50 W or less, with low heat production remove the need for an internal fan in many cases. Much cheaper lenses and therefore more
viewers with dual lens facility provide switching capacity between
reduction ratios; 24:1 for microfiche books and journals and 42:1 for
computer output microfiche data.

Turning to the subject of reduction ratios. It is a law of mathematics that space economy proceeds by squares of a linear reduction
size, and therefore there is a temptation to reduce beyond acceptable levels. This is now in abeyance with no development in the use
of ultrafiche, which suits library usage.

Other trends in microform equipment are the projection on wall
or desk facility. The screens on fast automatic retrieval units darken
in the transit of the film in order to avoid eye strain and reader-
printers have now moved into the plain paper copier era. Many of
these beneficial trends are relevant to the ergonomic aspects of the
use of screens in the other information technologies. In all types of
equipment the librarian needs to be vigilant to maintain high levels
of legibility. Business equipment manufacturers, as we have noted,
offer quite astonishingly small screens on some office automation
equipment. We are not concerned in libraries with what is discernible with effort. For sustained reading from any screen the image
must be at least the same size as the original. In this connection one
needs to observe the actual area of the screen used for display. On

VDUs it is often significantly less than appears to be the case at first glance. All screens too, must be adjustable for height and angle.

Siting of facilities

In order to seek optimum use of expensive facilities, it is desirable not to have a separate microform, optical and electronic media reading room. Suitable areas of general reading rooms are more likely to be effective. In a library with large open plan floor areas with natural illumination on all sides, the reading areas adjacent to the central service core should be selected. In libraries of different basic plan, similar areas, low on natural lighting but readily accessible and apparent to all library users are ideal.

These facilities need to be provided within the periodicals reading room, within main subject reading rooms for books, within a reference-information area and in catalogue and bibliography areas. Separate accommodation (air conditioned) should be provided for storage of archival material, and for television/video/audio viewing and listening. One should bear in mind that all these materials and equipment are best used and stored at temperatures not exceeding 70°F with 40% humidity. The library environment, of course, is one with a total ban on eating, drinking and smoking and so major hazards are not present.

Non-book reading areas require chairs of adjustable height and angle. Some tables should be divided on a carrel basis for those who prefer them, but most tables are likely to be unencumbered with partitions to allow free movement of machines as necessary. It should be possible to vary the lighting for different parts of the room, as users have differing needs as to ambient light. There should, of course, be an adequate number of electrical power points.

Policy matters

It is necessary to adopt a positive attitude to the acquisition of microform and electronic based services in libraries. Each should be selected on its merits as the most cost effective means of supplying the library user *conveniently* with the available information.

Library staff should never apologise to readers because the required material is available only on-line or only in microform, but should have a positive attitude resulting from observation that there is a sound policy in operation rather than haphazard acquisition of this and that. Staff need to be thoroughly aware of what is stocked in each type of non-book provision and trained in its retrieval for use. Those in charge of these materials should be responsible professional librarians with an empathy for automated systems.

The equipment should be regularly serviced and should be the best that can be had for the money available, with due regard to the ergonomic requirements stated previously. Old equipment should be written off. In addition to regular servicing, weekly cleaning procedures should be enforced. The minimum equipment necessary is that which will enable the efficient and comfortable reading of each non-book format. There is no single piece of equipment that will enable this, even for all the microformats, for the needs of each are different.

Therefore one needs a variety of equipment, but variety does not indicate an indecisive approach, for the whole information technology industry is a rapidly developing area of innovation, and it is wise to have a rolling programme of equipment purchase. The worst method of proceeding is to consult and purchase from only one manufacturer or supplier. One should visit other libraries and examine the equipment in use. Library objectives should be determined and appropriate systems purchased to serve those purposes.

Machine phobia

There will be librarians who have an in-built tendency to fear that they cannot cope with electronic devices. For their benefit, it must be stressed that information technology is becoming very much a consciously consumer-orientated industry. Equipment is now designed to be 'user-friendly', with keyboards labelled with words like 'run', 'store' or 'list', with 'menus' of choices displayed on the screen and add-on touch screens available further to ease the user's task.

There had long been a need to remove the barrier effect of confronting the non-technically minded librarian or library client with devices requiring some skill in prising data from their mass-produced impersonal keyboards and screens. This has been achieved by what must be the simplest human being/machine interface, the touch screen visual display unit. This is equivalent to scanning the index of a book and turning to the correct page, except that the page is turned by a touch on the screen.

At the library/user end, increasingly, no knowledge of computing will be assumed, operation will become a matter of plugging in an operating system disc and switching on. To date, computerised library systems have been planned with data processing in mind, for purposes of catalogue and issue systems automation and sharpening up existing book based retrieval systems.

The next step, as we have noted above, must be information systems planned from the outset for their specific library purpose of providing information on request — a one-stage process. These will be neither book substitute nor library substitute innovations but devices which, when fully exploited, will perform additional library services that proved to be not possible before their advent. They will certainly be such that even those with machine phobia can happily use them.

References

1   *Anglo-American Cataloguing Rules*; 2nd ed., prepared by the American Library Association, the British Library, the Canadian Committee on Cataloguing, the Library Association, the Library of Congress; edited by Michael Gorman and Paul W. Winkler. Library Association (1978)
2   COX, J. 'UK Video producers and distributors', *Int. J. Micrographics & Video Technology*, 3, 1 (1984) 15–22
3   FELLMAN, T. H., *et al*, 'An ergonomic evaluation of VDTs' by T. H. Fellman, U. Brauninger, R. Gierer and E. Grandjean, *Behaviour and Information Technology*, 1, 1, (1982) pp. 69–80

Eleven

Convergent technologies

If we are to apply the best technique to each aspect of information transfer, information technologies have to be seen as convergent technologies. All these technologies are needed. We are concerned with document storage and retrieval *and also* the storage and retrieval of *information* that has never been and might never be in *document* form.

The role of each technology is fairly clear. Microforms are ideal for housing as much material as possible on the spot in a library. Space saving has been estimated as being up to 95% of the space taken up by equivalent printed materials. However, it must be remembered that the information technologies, without exception, require reading 'stations' in the library. Each user of non-book material requires rather more space than does a reader of a printed book. Regarding handling costs, 2000 pages of A4 paper weigh 16 lb, the same number of pages reproduced on 16 mm roll film weigh 4oz and on microfiche 1 oz; thus physical handling of microforms could be cheaper. However, whilst a library of books is likely to be perfectly suitable for self-service on open access, we know from experience that microform usage will require more staff.

As to archival quality, silver halide film will ensure longevity whereas modern papers will not, unless they are top quality and hand made. For catalogues, computer output microfiche provides a cheap regularly updated record that we can no longer afford to attempt to achieve on cards in any but the smallest library.

Ever since the 1930s and until quite recently the motive force for microform provision has not been the need for space economy in libraries but rather the escalating pressures for conservation of the materials of research and the records of our intellectual heritage. These pressures have been closely associated with the development of the major non-book element present in libraries — microfilm.

Colour microfilm remains the best means of obtaining faithful representation of coloured original material. However, as colour film dyes fade, refilming may be necessary from time to time.

Printed bound volumes will remain the staple of library provision at least until well into the next century. Less frequently used material will be stored after conversion to one of the archival microform formats. Journals and other periodical publications will be used in the year of publication in print on paper format, but instead of being bound into volumes, microform storage will become the norm.

Prophecy is dangerous, as the convergence of information technologies will produce even better ways of handling certain sorts of data. It is possible that longevity of the electronic storage media will improve; first to ensure medium term survival and, later on, long-term survival. In the meanwhile, copying of discs and tapes, magnetic and optical, will be a necessary part of an information provider's operation.

Convergence of the main frame computer and micrographics technologies provided us with the computer output microfiche catalogue as well as computer-assisted retrieval from data bases held on microfiche and film. Convergence of the technologies of telecommunications, main frame and microcomputers gave us the facility of on-line searching.

Laser optical data disc technology married to computer assisted retrieval will make data bank in place of data base searching a developing information field. Data banks will be purpose built with the needs of library users in mind. Whilst, in all probability, digital optical disc storage will replace micrographic storage in on-line systems, it will not do so in off-line systems because of the low cost of micrographic input and output devices compared with those based on laser optic and digital equipment.

As we have just stated prophecy is dangerous, but, nevertheless a recent study chanced the following forecasts:[1]

'By the year 2000, 50% of existing indexing/abstracting services will be available only in electronic form. The 90% level of conversion will not be reached until later. Existing periodicals (in science and technology, social sciences and the humanities) will not reach even the 25% level of conversion until after 2000.

By 1990, 25% of existing reference books will only be available in electronic form. The 50% level of conversion will only occur after the year 2000. By 1995, 50% of newly issued technical reports will only be available in electronic form. The 90% level will be reached after the year 2000.

When it is considered that these comments refer only to research literature, they reinforce the view that the vast majority of publications will continue to appear in conventional form for at least 20 years from now.

Conclusion

Print on paper must be regarded as just one of the physical media which carry information. Other media are microfilm, magnetic tape, magnetic disc, video tape, video disc, electromagnetic waves, pulses of light in fibre optic cables, etc. If, as I have stressed, librarianship is the profession concerned with the acquisition and exploitation of information for use, then all the products of the *new technology*, (such as computers, main-frame, micro and mini, facsimile transmitters, word-processors, video recorders, etc.) are potential producers of the new materials of librarianship.

Information technology involves the application of these new technology devices to information transfer. They constitute additional ways of handling information to those presented by the book, the printed journal and the microform. They are themselves microform in the sense that what is handled is not printed symbols or words conveying the information but digital or analogue representations of it. Thus there is physical space saving in storage. Also, handling and storage being combined in computer applications there is saving on staff in the longer term.

It is worthy of note that the electronic office concept, in spite of considerable promotion, has so far failed to win more than a very limited acceptance. The paper-based office remains the means by which business and administrative activities are operated, because of its general efficiency and its familiarity, as well as the conservatism of management and staff. The real potential of the electronic office lies in its ability to perform additional tasks to provide more information more quickly by using only one set of data, processed in various ways, for all the activities of an organisation.

To be effective, therefore, one needs a total system developed after detailed systems analysis of all the activities. Present reality is characterised by piecemeal introduction of unrelated items of information technology equipment in the various divisions of an organisation. Often the pieces of equipment are incompatible with each other.

Not surprisingly, this has proved to be similar in the library context with unrelated purchases of electronic typewriters, word processors, microcomputers, microform reader-printers, on-line information systems terminals and computerised issue systems unrelated to computerised cataloguing systems. The efficient approach now requires a system that enables the entering of data once only at the time of first ordering a book with the same data thereafter used for accessioning, cataloguing, issue records, recall notices, stock control, reservations, analysis of expenditure and of usage by subject, etc. All this should be an integrated system on totally compatible equipment.

Given that we eventually arrive at this situation, then the work of the librarian could be affected by the ability and willingness of library users to spend much more of their time at home in their electronic office environment and increasingly call up information online.

The role of engineering in information technology is not a problem, but the role of the librarian, if not a problem, needs to be carefully stated. The best technical means available must be used in libraries for each process of information transfer and this involves regular updating of equipment. The quality of information, that is to say its faithfulness in representing the text as written, its currency, that is its completeness to that point in time and its intelligibility to the user, are vital. Its cost is heavily influenced by the intellectual effort content and the equipment necessary to input, store, retrieve and read the information, plus, the library overheads. The charges involved will only be met by the user, directly or indirectly, if, over a period of time, they represent his or her conception of the value gained.

The librarian is not only the gatekeeper to the information available through the library, but also the co-ordinator of the user evaluation of the performance of information services. As such, the librarian must be totally unbiased in professional practice and a manager of a vital human resource — information, whether it be in books or any of the many media we have discussed.

Reference

1 LANCASTER, F. W., *et al*, 'The impact of a paperless society on the research library of the future'. Final report to the National Science Foundation. University of Illinois, Graduate School of Library Science, 1980.

Suggestion for Further Reading

DOWLIN, K. E., *The Electronic Library: the promise and the process.* 199 pp. Neal Schuman/Mansell Publishing Ltd. (1984).

Glossary

Alphanumeric A set of data containing both letters and figures.

Analogue computer One in which magnitudes are represented by physical variations such as current, or resistance, or voltage.

Analogue recording Representation of data by variations in current, or voltage, or resistance, or reflectance, etc.

Aperture card A card that can be sorted mechanically or electronically, housing a frame or frames of exposed film set into an aperture or apertures in the card.

Archival quality The ability of an entire processed film or print ro retain its original characteristics during prolonged use and storage. The ability of any information medium to retain its characteristics.

Audio disc A disc carrying music, speech, etc, recorded electro-magnetically, optically or by any other technique.

Audio tape A tape carrying music, speech, etc, recorded electro-magnetically.

Batch processing A computer operating method in which the data are accumulated and processed one after another.

Baud The unit used to express the speed of data transmission over telephone or other landlines (bits per second).

Bit The smallest unit of information that a computer handles. It represents either 1 or 0.

Byte Eight bits, or one alphanumeric character. The capacity of computer storage is measured in kilobytes or megabytes.

Cartridge A single-core enclosed container of processed roll microfilm (16 mm or 35 mm). When loaded on an appropriate viewer, the film is automatically threaded on to a take-up spool built into the viewer.

Cassette A double-core enclosed container of processed roll microfilm (16 mm). It encloses both supply and take-up spool in a single case.

Chip A small piece of material, normally silicon, that holds thousands of electronic circuits.

Ciné mode Jargon term denoting the orientation of micro-images with the bottom of each frame adjacent to the top of the succeeding frame. Vertical mode.

COM Computer output microfilm or computer output microfiche. Computer held machine readable digital data is converted and directly output onto microfilm as textual or graphical information.

Comic mode Jargon term denoting the orientation of micro-images with the right hand edge of each frame adjacent to the left hand edge of the succeeding frame. Horizontal mode.

Computer An electronic device that accepts data, stores it, and outputs information that is the result of the application of logical processes to that data. Thus it consists of an input device, a central processing unit, a memory and an output device.

Contrast The relationship between high and low density areas of a photographic image or screen display.

Data transfer rate The speed of transfer of data into or out of the computer memory. Measured in kilobytes or megabytes per second.

Data transmission equipment Data transmission equipment operates in one of several ways:
> One character at a time
> One line at a time
> One data block at a time
> Synchronous – controlled by a clock
> Asynchronous – untimed
> Duplex – sending and receiving simultaneously or on one line.

Density	The light-absorbing quality of a photographic image. The greater the absorption, the higher the density.
Diazo process	A method of microfilm duplication in which film having a diazonium salt emulsion is exposed to ultraviolet light transmitted through a master microfilm and then processed in ammonia vapour.
Digital computer	One in which data are represented by digits rather than physical quantities.
Digital recording	Data recording using two symbols 'one' and 'nought' or 'on' and 'off' manipulated in an electronic circuit by pre-determined logic.
Digitiser	Equipment that converts graphical or textual information directly into digital data for computer input or line transmission.
Disc drive	Computer equipment purpose-built for 'floppy', hard, single or double-sided discs. (All terms self explanatory).
Electronic publishing	The production and dissemination of information via electronic media from the author using a word processor or microcomputer to the reader on-line at a visual display unit. Ideally it includes payment by electronic transfer of funds and remote provision of printed copy electronically.
Facsimile transmission equipment	Equipment that scans and converts to electrical impulses and sends over telephone lines to a converter at the other end.
Fiche-book	A bound volume with a printed book element and a major microfiche component.
Generation	The original film in the camera is a first generation microfilm, a duplicate made from it is a second generation copy and so on. The same term is used to indicate the relationship of a disc to the master pressing.
Information technology	The convergence of the technologies of computers, telecommunications and micrographics with microelectronics as the facilitator.

Jacket microfilm   A transparent plastic carrier with a sleeve or sleeves to hold exposed microfilm.

Laser recording   A method of recording using light amplification by stimulated emission of radiation.

Local area network   A line network of computers in an area used for high speed data communication.

Magnetic disc   High volume, high speed storage medium (magnetised bits) giving random or direct accessibility.

Magnetic tape   High speed input output medium that stores data in the form of magnetised bits. Serial accessibility, not random.

Magnification ratio   Magnification expressed as a ratio (as 1:24), where the measurement of a given linear dimension of a displayed micro-image is compared with the corresponding linear dimension of the microimage itself.

Main-frame computer   A large computer of great capability, requiring specialist operators and a controlled environment.

Memory   The memory of a computer is its random access storage capacity available for use. It is measured in megabytes.

Microcard   A registered name for one type of opaque microform.

Microcomputer   A computer normally designed for the individual user, personal or business. The distinction between micros and minis has become blurred. A microcomputer handles 8, 6, or 32 bits.

Microfiche   A sheet of processed film, usually 105 mm × 148 mm bearing microimages in a grid pattern and a 'header strip' with identification legible to the unaided eye.

Microfilm   A high resolution film of fine grain for recording microimages.

Microform   A medium, normally photographic film, storing information, textual, illustrative or tabular, at reduced size, illegible to the unaided human eye.

Micrographics   Activities relating to the creation and use of microforms.

Micro-opaque	A card of opaque material bearing micro-images, photographic or photolithographic, on one or both sides, with identification details legible to the unaided eye. Read by reflectance and enlargement.
Microprint	A registered name for one type of opaque microform.
Micropublishing	Publishing in microform.
Mini-computer	A computer larger and more powerful than a micro. It may need a controlled environment to operate efficiently. Handles 16, 32 or even 48 bits.
Modem	A modulator–demodulator used to connect a computer to a telephone line (usually a dedicated line for obvious reasons). In transmitting, the digital signals from the computer become analogue modulations of the telephone current. In receiving, it converts the analogue signals from the telephone to digital pulses for the computer.
Multiplexer	A device that accepts several inputs and transmits them simultaneously.
Negative	A photographic image that appears light against a dark background.
On-line	A mode of operation with immediate access to a remote computer by terminal.
Optical character recognition	Computer input directly from the original document without an intermediary keyboard. The kind of characters that can be read will depend upon the OCR device hardware *and* its software.
Optical disc	Effectively a video disc that uses an optical technology such as a laser beam, where the reading head does not have mechanical contact with the disc.
Planetary camera	Photographic equipment in which the document remains stationary on a plane surface during filming.
Plotter	Device for printing graphical information from a computer file directly onto paper, film or glass plates.

Positive   A photographic image that appears dark against a light background.

Printer, data output   A device to output up to 12 copies of computer held data onto paper (uses special paper).

Reduction ratio   Linear dimension of the microimage expressed in relation to the linear dimension of the original (as 1:16).

Resolution   A measure of the capability of a film to record fine detail and of a viewer, VDU or other screen to enable easy reading of fine detail.

Roll film   The generic name for reel, spool or cassette microfilm.

Screen size   The size quoted for VDU and television screens is a diagonal measurement in inches. The characters per line and lines per screen are vital measurements.

Silver halide film   Film with photo-sensitive silver compounds (of chlorine, bromine, fluorine, etc). When processed a metallic silver 'archival' image results.

Simultaneous edition   Publication simultaneously in print and microform.

Speed of operation (computers)   Measured either in clock speed (millions of cycles per second) as MHz, the higher the better, or cycle time (nano-seconds) as nsec, the shorter the better.

Step and repeat camera   This type of camera automatically moves sheet film, normally 105 mm, through the camera at each step photographing one frame, in a progression along each row.

Synoptic journal   A printed periodical publication carrying only summary articles with the full text contained on a microfiche within.

Teletext   Information system using television broadcasts to carry public data services.

Telex   Transmitter-receiver for text over land lines. Consists of keyboard and printer and sometimes a screen. Terminals can be mechanical or electronic.

Touch screen	A visual display unit screen with a sensitive overlay that enables selection from displayed options by a touch. It obviates the need for ability to use a keyboard.
Ultrafiche	Ultra high reduction microfiche (above 1:90). Can carry up to 3000 pages of images.
Vesicular film	When exposed optical vesicles or bubbles are produced in the light-sensitive part which is in suspension in a plastic layer. The imperfections form the latent image made visible by heating and cooling.
Video disc	A disc carrying ultrafine recording impressions, that, when played on a special turntable interfaced with a television set, provides pictures and sound or text.
Video tape	A tape recording medium carrying sound and pictures that is played back via equipment interfaced with a television receiver.
Videotext	Information system using the telephone network for private or public data services, with a visual display unit terminal.
Viewdata	See Videotext.
Word processor	Equipment for the origination, storage, editing and output of 'typed' text. They range from electronic typewriters to computerised systems. Properly comprise keyboard, display screen, memory, processing unit and printer.
Word size	The number of bits a computer can store in its memory or retrieve in a single operation.

Index